WW1 at Sea

www.pocketessentials.com

Other Pocket Essentials by the same author:

Nelson

WW1 at Sea

VICTORIA CAROLAN

POCKET ESSENTIALS

This edition published in 2007 by Pocket Essentials
P.O.Box 394, Harpenden, Herts, AL5 1XJ
www.pocketessentials.com

ISBN 978-1-84243-212-9

2 4 6 8 10 9 7 5 3 1

Typeset by Avocet Typeset, Chilton, Aylesbury, Bucks
Printed and bound in Great Britain by J.H. Haynes Ltd, Sparkford, Somerset

This book is dedicated to my great friend Lucy Smith
who has seen me through thick and thin.

Acknowledgements

My grateful thanks go to Chris Ware who has supported me through every stage of this book with good humour and indispensable advice.

I would also like to thank my editor, Nick Rennison, for his expertise and patience both on this book and my previous publication on Nelson. Thanks also to Ion and Claire at Pocket Essentials.

Contents

Introduction

Images of WWI in the popular consciousness normally involve the bloody attrition of trench warfare, the miles of mud, the shattered earth, the tangled miles of barbed wire. However, there was another significant arena of war – the battle for control of the sea. The war at sea has received less attention partly because it is less immediately dramatic. The Royal Navy had to play a long game in sustaining the distant blockade that would eventually cripple Germany. The Navy provided the screen which enabled the war on land.

In 1914, at the beginning of the war, Britain's maritime supremacy had remained unchallenged for around a hundred years. Many expected another Battle of Trafalgar but advances in technology saw a very different kind of warfare with the widespread use of mines, submarines and torpedoes. There was a steep learning curve as the impact of the new technology was initially underestimated by both sides and neither side had experience of command in fleet action. The experience of the First World War would do much to inform the Second World War, particularly in the use of aviation.

The war at sea affected every ocean in the world, and in a book of this size it is impossible to consider all the smaller conflicts in every arena. The book examines the events that led to war and the naval arms race between Britain and Germany. It traces the events of the war at sea, looking at the major battles, the effects of unrestricted submarine warfare and some of the key protagonists.

The War Begins

Victory at the Battle of Trafalgar and the defeat of Napoleon at Waterloo saw the start of an era in which Britain's maritime supremacy was virtually unchallenged for nearly a hundred years. However, as the nineteenth century drew to a close, Britain's Empire was beginning to feel the strain, with war in South Africa and increasing tension over the question of Home Rule in Ireland. None the less, Britain in 1900 was still the wealthiest nation in the world. She was dependent on her sea power for world trade and to import sufficient food to feed a densely populated island. It was essential that she maintained her maritime supremacy and fear of losing it was to become a dominant feature of the early twentieth century.

The Background to the Build Up to War

Tensions were beginning to mount throughout Europe from the 1890s onwards and these years saw an intensification of ambitious nationalism that would ultimately lead to the outbreak of World War One. The balance between the major European powers started to shift with the rise of the German Empire. Successful wars in 1866 against the Austrian Empire and against France in 1870 saw the unification of German states with the Kingdom of Prussia to create what was the most powerful empire in Europe. The Dual Monarchy of Austria-Hungary was also an ally to Germany.

Even as late as the 1890s, Britain perceived her old enemy France as her biggest rival. The belief was not entirely without foundation. After its humiliating losses to Germany, the French army turned to Africa which brought it into conflict with British interests. In addition, the French navy had been keeping abreast of new technology and in some cases had introduced it ahead of Britain. In fact, the Royal Navy was the only major maritime power not to have submarines by 1900, although there were plans for their introduction. Britain's other fear in the nineteenth century was France's major ally, the Russian Empire, whose expansion endangered British routes into India through the Middle East. In order to protect these routes into India, Britain supported the Turkish Empire. Russia's ambitions in the East were halted when they were defeated by Japan in the war of 1904–5 and they turned instead towards the Ottoman Empire. Slav communities in Greece, Serbia and Bulgaria traditionally looked to Russia for support. Austria-Hungary became increasingly fearful of its own minority Slav population as Russia encouraged Slav independence.

Britain was alarmed when Russia and France signed the Dual Entente in 1891. A solution to the country's anxieties may have been to ally herself with Germany but Britain was unwilling to make such a commitment, German diplomacy failed and, most importantly, Germany's naval programme was a direct threat to Britain. Britain was aware that her maritime supremacy was under threat and made an alliance with Japan in 1902. This was the first union that Britain had made for nearly a hundred years. In 1904, Britain put aside her recent problems with France over Africa and entered into the so-called *Entente Cordiale*, although this was not a formal alliance. In 1907, after Japan defeated Russia, Britain settled the border disputes in Persia and Afghanistan with Russia and formed the *Triple Entente* with the Tsarist Empire and with France. The agreement did not commit Britain to provide military support in the event of war but, when Germany attempted to undermine France's influence in Morocco with a show of naval might in 1911, Britain made her backing of France more explicit. As a result it became clearer that, in the event of war, Britain would most likely provide military support to the *Entente*.

War between Germany and Britain began to look more likely, as Germany stepped up its naval expansion and, at the same time, relations between Russia and Austria-Hungary worsened. In 1908, Austria annexed Bosnia-Herzegovina and the then Serb government set up a liberation movement that included the covert terrorist group called the Black Hand. With Russian support, Serbia formed the Balkan League with Greece, Bulgaria and Montenegro. The primary aim was to remove the Turks from the Balkan peninsula and the first Balkan war started in 1912, at a time when the Turks were also defending their lands in Libya from the Italians who had grand plans to expand their own empire. The countries in the Balkan League were victorious but, in 1913, they fought a second war between themselves over the gains. Serbia's successes led to great fears in Austria which reached their zenith with the assassination in Sarajevo of the heir to the Austrian throne, Archduke Franz Ferdinand, on 28 July 1914. His assassin was Gavril Princip, a young member of the Black Hand.

Austria's primary concern now was to destroy the Serbian enemy for good. Knowing that Russia would come out in support of Serbia, the Austrians first made sure that Germany would support them and then they issued an ultimatum to Serbia. The ultimatum was ignored and so Austria declared war on 28 July. Russia, unwilling to abandon Serbia, mobilised on 30 July and her ally France, equally unwilling to abandon Russia, planned to follow suit. Russian mobilisation was followed by German mobilisation. Germany's plan was to invade Belgium and to hope for a quick victory over France so that the French would be unable to mobilise in support of Russia. It was the invasion of Belgium that drew Britain into the war, because an implicit part of British naval policy since the sixteenth century had been that the Low Countries should not fall into enemy hands. When the British government's request for Belgian neutrality to be respected received no answer, Britain declared war on Germany on 4 August 1914.

The Naval Arms Race 1890–1914

The years leading up to the First World War saw a period of intense navalism throughout Europe, and Britain was no exception. There had never been a period when the concerns and armament of the Royal Navy figured more highly in the public sphere. Organisations such as the Navy Records Society and the Navy League began to flourish and there were numerous naval exhibitions. Alfred Thayer Mahan's *The Influence of Seapower on History* was published at this time, and its ideas partly effected the decisions of other nations to begin building modern fleets of their own in the hope that they could wield the kind of influence that Britain had across the world. Japan was one of the first nations to take up the maritime challenge and Britain set up a naval mission in Tokyo in 1882 to aid them. Theodore Roosevelt was an enthusiastic supporter of Mahan and so led America to build up her own navy, seeing its expansion as the key to world power. However, there was no keener disciple of Mahan than Germany's Kaiser Wilhelm who had long envied the navy of his grandmother, Queen Victoria.

The experience of the Russo-Japanese War of 1904–1905, when the Japanese wiped out the Russian fleet at the battle of Tsuchima, demonstrated to the world that, with the threat from mines and torpedoes, it made sense to greatly extend the range at which battleships fought each other. It was seen that Russian battleships could accurately fire over 18,000 yards. The common practice at this time in the Royal Navy was to target at around 3,000 yards but future battles, it was clear, would be fought at ranges of five to ten miles, and this meant that battleships would be best armed with long-range 12-inch guns, supported by flotillas of torpedo boats. Admiral John (Jacky) Fisher, who had just been appointed First Sea Lord in 1904, almost immediately set designers to work to create what would become HMS *Dreadnought*, launched in February 1906. *Dreadnought* was armed with ten 12-inch guns, double the number of any other vessel, and could reach speeds of 21 knots which was, on average, three knots faster than most battleships. The launch of the *Dreadnought* effectively made all other battleships obsolete and forced the German Admiral, von Tirpitz, to suspend his ship-building programme so that the German navy could begin its own plans for dreadnought-class vessels. It ultimately intensified the Anglo-German naval race.

There was great excitement in Britain over the *Dreadnought*, although Fisher's critics were concerned about not only the enormous cost of building it but also the cost of replacement if it was lost, especially since Fisher had actually been appointed to make cuts in naval spending. Nevertheless she inspired a class of vessel that became known universally as the dreadnought and very soon the navies of the world were designing their own versions. Fisher was a very controversial figure and the many reforms that he introduced between 1904 and 1909, which essentially modernised the Royal Navy, made him many enemies. He was ruthless in taking older vessels out of service (many of them were used again during the war) or scrapping them but he also reformed recruitment, training and introduced naval reserves, all of which would prove important in fighting World War One. He was largely responsible for the creation of a submarine service at a time when many felt that submarines were weapons of dirty warfare and not quite 'British'. Britain had previously maintained her navy with the expectation that her major rivals would be France and Russia, but now they were forced to respond to the German expansion.

The rise of the German Navy was remarkable. The first Navy Act was passed in 1898 and, within little more than a decade, the Germans built the second largest battle fleet in the world from scratch, largely under Admiral Alfred von Tirpitz. The realisation of the necessity to respond to Germany culminated in 1909 with the biggest peacetime naval scare that Britain had had in her history. Intelligence in London reported that there was to be a further acceleration in the German building of dreadnoughts. Also, the improvements and expansion of German shipbuilding meant that they could build approximately eight dreadnoughts per year, thus equalling the British capacity. This information led to a huge debate in Parliament over the 1909 naval estimates (budget) and over the question of whether four or six new dreadnoughts should be built. The radical Liberals, including Lloyd George and Winston Churchill, argued that the nation could only afford four ships, and that the Admiralty was being alarmist in wanting more. The Conservatives fought for six ships. Prime Minister Asquith brokered a solution that ironically would provide for eight new vessels – four to be built in 1909–10 and provision for a further four vessels if it proved necessary. The decision was prompted by further intelligence that Germany's ally, Austria, had begun plans for three or four dreadnoughts. This, in turn, had caused concern in Italy which had immediately begun its own building programme.

For Fisher, however, dreadnoughts were very much a deterrent to the Germans rather than necessarily a decisive instrument of war and he was perceptive in realising that the submarine and torpedo would come to be as important in naval warfare. Fisher was confident that Britain could maintain her advantage over Germany in the strength of her fleet and, indeed, this was true. However, it was clear that it was becoming too costly for Britain to maintain her fleets throughout the world and Fisher began to concentrate on deployments in home waters. The Mediterranean Fleet was very much reduced and, when Churchill became First Lord of the Admiralty in October 1911, he intended to take this reduction even further. The French moved their only battleship squadron from Brest to the Mediterranean. Many took this to be the result of an agreement Britain had made in advance with France under the *Entente Cordiale* but, in reality, the French had reached the decision separately. Essentially, the move left the French to guard the Mediterranean and the British with only a small force at Gibraltar, though enough that the combined Anglo-French force would outnumber the Italian and Austrian fleets.

In 1912, Churchill revealed in Parliament that Britain

was no longer maintaining the long-held policy of the two-power standard, meaning that the British fleet should be superior to the combined force of her two most powerful rivals. Now the fleet was to be built to ensure superiority over Germany alone. There were some efforts around this time to halt the naval race with Germany (for example, Churchill's proposal that both countries should suspend further shipbuilding for a year) but all diplomacy eventually failed. In fact, technological advances intensified the race even further with the development of the superdreadnought which carried 15-inch guns.

The Early Stages of War

The mobilisation of the Navy went very efficiently and there was the added bonus that there had been a major exercise for reservists in the summer of 1914. They were about to be dispersed but, with the outbreak of war, they were detained and therefore ready for action almost immediately. The British Grand Fleet (previously known as the First Fleet) with twenty dreadnoughts and four battle cruisers was sent to its war station, Scapa Flow in the Orkneys, to prevent German entry into the North Sea. The commander-in-chief was the newly appointed Sir John Jellicoe who had been a previous Director of Naval Ordnance and Controller of the Navy. He replaced a devastated Sir John Callaghan at the last minute on 4 August, and had been Fisher's preferred candidate for some time. Also to the north there were two patrols, the Sixth Cruiser

Squadron with four *Drake* class vessels and the Tenth Cruiser Squadron with eight *Edgar* class cruisers. In the Channel was Vice Admiral Sir Cecil Burney's fleet with eighteen pre-dreadnoughts and four light cruisers. Off Harwich, Commodore Reginald Tyrwhitt was in command of thirty-five destroyers and two light cruisers, as well as sixteen *D* and *E* class submarines under Commodore Roger Keyes in the Eighth Submarine Flotilla. In addition, Keyes was in command of the Sixth Submarine Flotilla comprising six older vessels. There were also smaller forces at the Nore, Portsmouth and Devonport. Rear Admiral George Ballard was the admiral of patrols and commanded forces, generally made up of older vessels, to protect the east coast and the shipping lanes to and from France. However, the majority of cruisers in the Channel were French, and it had been agreed in 1913 that, should France and Britain be allies in war, the French would protect the western side between the Contentin Peninsula and England and the Royal Navy would be responsible for the straits of Dover.

Merchant ships were also an important part of British defences and more than 200 were requisitioned for blockade duties, in addition to a small number of armoured vessels, in the first months of the war. By the end of the war the number had grown to 3,700 merchant vessels involved in auxiliary patrol.

The High Seas Fleet, Germany's strongest naval force, was based in the North Sea under the command of Admiral Ingenohl. Two squadrons (1st and 3rd), comprising eight older dreadnoughts and four new *Konig* class dreadnoughts (with plans for another two to join), were based at the mouth of the Jade River in northwest Germany with entry into the North Sea. Also based at Jade River was a group of four battle cruisers under the command of Rear Admiral Franz Hipper who was the senior officer in charge of scouting groups. The Second Squadron, with eight pre-dreadnoughts, was based at the mouth of Elbe. Both river mouths were protected by a number of lighter vessels and two submarine flotillas, made up of nineteen vessels, were attached to the High Seas Fleet. Other groups, generally with older vessels, were being assembled for the Baltic and were commanded separately by Prince Heinrich of Prussia, brother to the Kaiser.

At the beginning of war, many people expected that there would be a major sea battle within the first few days with a decisive victory to rival Trafalgar. However, it was immediately obvious at the outset of war that the traditional British tactic of close blockade was impractical. The technological breakthroughs of torpedoes, submarines, mines and long-range costal defences meant that it was too dangerous to blockade at close quarters. In addition, ships would have to return to port every three to four days to coal and, depending on the distance to a home port, a blockade might require three squadrons – one to blockade, one in port and one in transit – which would have needed more ships than were available. The strategy adopted was therefore a distant blockade. The Germans were surprised both by the speed of the British mobilisation and by the fact that a close blockade was not forthcoming, since much of their strategy had been predicated on that eventuality. They had also not been prepared for the fact that the British did not have a squadron patrolling Heligoland. The Germans had intended to grind down the anticipated close-blockading British Fleet with submarines and mines, rather than risking full battle, as they fully expected that the Grand Fleet would seize upon them as soon as they left port. They were also reluctant to risk full battle while the British maintained their numerical advantage in ships.

The British deployment, as long as it was able to hold, essentially blocked Germany from trading with the rest of the world and thereby also protected Britain's merchant fleet which, at around 19 million tons, accounted for nearly 50% of the world's total. The Channel, with its patrolling submarines and its mines, was too dangerous for an enemy to contemplate breaking through and this left the northern entry to the North Sea as the only real option for the Germans to get out. There were weaknesses in the defence at Scapa Flow because, should the Fleet venture out, there were no fully operational armed bases on the east coast. The anchorage at Scapa Flow itself was vulnerable to submarines and mines as well as to surface attack because it had no fixed guns, searchlights or nets to protect it.

The first major operation for the Royal Navy was to transport divisions of the British Expeditionary Force (BEF) to France which started on 7 August. Squadrons blocking routes into the Channel protected them. Before the war the Germans had hoped that they might hamper such transports by attacks on a British Fleet in close blockade, but when that did not materialise the only way that they could have made any impact was to use their battle fleet. This they were not prepared to risk. In addition, the Germans had great confidence in their Schlieffen Plan on land, which was essentially to conquer France swiftly before Russia could come to her aid, and they did not consider that the relatively small BEF would significantly affect the outcome. So the troops were landed in France unimpeded.

The first skirmish at sea occurred on the 5 August when the German minelayer *Königin Luise*, disguised as a passenger vessel (which in fact she had been before the war), was on a mission to lay mines off the port of Harwich. Admiral Tyrwhitt was patrolling the line between Harwich and Terschelling (in Dutch waters) and, on hearing intelligence of the minelayer's presence, dispatched the destroyers *Lance* and *Landrail* to investigate. The *Amphion* also joined them but it was *Lance* that fired the first shot of the war at sea. The minelayer was outnumbered, lightly armed and stood little chance. She was sunk with a loss of 54 out of her 100 crew. The very next day, *Amphion* was sunk by one of the mines that had been laid by the *Königin Luise*.

In the first weeks of the war U-boats were reaching Scapa Flow and as far as the Norwegian coast. The capacity of the submarines to travel such distances had been seriously underrated. There was a wake up call for the Royal

Navy when a submarine attacked the *Monarch* on gunnery practice less than 500 miles from Heligoland. When the German First Submarine Flotilla headed into the North Sea on 6 August, its men were still unaware of the exact location of the ships of the Grand Fleet which had not appeared, as expected, at Heligoland Bight. Two of the ten German submarines were lost, one disappeared and another rammed by the cruiser *Birmingham* and sunk with the loss of all crew. With awareness of the submarine danger heightened, there were false sightings and a couple of major scares that, in jest, came to be referred to as the first and second Battles of Scapa. However, there was genuine danger at Scapa Flow. In November *U.18* managed to enter Hoxa Sound, one of the entry points to the anchorage, although it was forced by a trawler to scuttle itself before it could attack. Through the submarine patrols, Admiral Ingenohl realised that British Forces were at the northern entrance to the North Sea and he decided on a policy of guerrilla-type warfare of raids into the British areas. This was not dissimilar to original German ideas, when they expected a close blockade, in that they intended to wear down the enemy gradually.

On 15 and 16 August the German light cruisers *Köln* and *Stuttgart*, accompanied by torpedo boats, were sent on reconnaissance around Heligoland Bight with a mission to attack British submarines thought to be in the area. Nothing came of this mission but the Germans were more successful on 18 August when the light cruisers *Stralsund* and *Strassburg*, with submarine support, again went to seek out British forces. They came across the light cruiser *Fearless* as well as 16 destroyers of the First Flotilla from the Harwich light force. The British sighted the *Stralsund* but they mistook her for the much more heavily-armed German vessel *Yorck* and, as a consequence, Captain Blunt called for backup. Although the German vessels were outnumbered, Blunt was worried about the vulnerability of his light vessels in the face of the *Yorck*, and so Tyrwhitt came out with the rest of the Harwich-based force. In the meantime, *Stralsund* had got wind of the trap into which she was being lured, reversed course and got away.

The Battle of Heligoland Bight

It was a frustrating incident and there was considerable frustration throughout the British fleet with the lack of action so far at sea. In the meantime, Keyes had been making reconnaissance around the Bight and had built up a good picture of the patterns of German defence. He made a proposal to attack and attempt to eliminate German patrols around the Bight. Consequently, on 12 August, Churchill ordered Captain Herbert Richmond (the Assistant Director of the Operations Division of the Naval War Staff) and Admiral Christian (Commander of the Southern Force) to plan a raid on Heligoland Bight. The Bight was of strategic importance to the Germans because of its proximity to their major waterways – the Elbe, Jade, Weser and Eider rivers where the High Seas Fleet was stationed. It was not the first time such a plan had been suggested but, as had happened before, nothing came of it. Jellicoe, as eager for action as Keyes and Tyrwhitt, also submitted another such plan, one that was more ambitious and was to include the Grand Fleet in a sweep of Heligoland Bight. However, it was decided to postpone any plans for the moment because the transports of the BEF were still going across the Channel and Keyes was needed to protect them.

It was only on 24 August that Churchill called another meeting to put together final plans for the raid. The core force would include Tyrwhitt's entire Harwich Force and Keyes' eight submarines and two destroyers. Support was to be provided by the battle cruisers *Invincible* and *New Zealand*, stationed at the Humber under the command of Rear Admiral Sir Archibald Moore, and Rear Admiral Christian's Seventh Cruiser Squadron. This last squadron was of concern to Keyes and Tyrwhitt because it comprised of old Bacchante class ships which were to be stationed off Terschelling to intercept any enemy vessels. These were so slow that the Admirals doubted that they would be effective and worried about their vulnerability. Keyes requested the support of the stronger units – Commodore William Goodenough's First Light Cruiser Squadron and Vice Admiral David Beatty's First Battle Cruiser Squadron. His requests for both were turned down. As a result, Tyrwhitt and Keyes, briefing their captains about the forthcoming raid, informed them that the only British ships larger than a destroyer involved would be Tyrwhitt's light cruisers.

This was to have near-fatal consequences during the eventual battle.

On 25 August, a decision was taken to transport 3,000 Royal Marines to Ostend to protect the Belgian coast from the fast-approaching German Army. Churchill saw that the raid on Heligoland could also act as a diversion to any response that the High Seas Fleet might make to the movement of the marines. The raid therefore became a more significant operation. Communications between the Admiralty, Naval War Staff and the Commander-in-Chief of Navy were slow and inefficient and the source of constant criticism during the first years of the war. Jellicoe did not hear of the plans for the raid until 26 August which was the same day that the forces were to sortie in preparation for attack. His opinion was that there would not be sufficient strength to counteract an attack from a heavy German warship and so he offered his support; the Admiralty turned this down but said that he might send some battle cruisers if it was convenient. Jellicoe went a little further in dispatching Beatty's First Battle Cruiser Squadron as well as Commodore Goodenough's light cruisers, the support that Keyes had originally wanted. However, Tyrwhitt and Keyes did not receive the information in time for the start of the Battle of Heligoland on 28 August.

Tyrwhitt was to lead his 1st and 2nd Flotillas (32 cruisers) and his two light cruisers *Fearless* and *Arethusa* (his flagship that had been commissioned only two days before) in attack. Keyes was to form his submarines into two lines, one to attack German cruisers and one to draw cruisers away from the Bight and out to sea. Another pair of submarines was to guard the mouth of the Ems. Rear Admiral Archibald Moore was to cruise to the north with *New Zealand* and *Invincible*, should heavier support be required, and the old Bacchantes were off Terschelling as planned.

For the duration of the battle, which took place in haze and fog, visibility was poor and, to add to the confusion, there was the mix-up in communications. In light of the instructions received that there would only be Tyrwhitt's cruisers in the vicinity, there was enormous bewilderment at the arrival of Goodenough's cruisers. Tyrwhitt recognised them as he was beginning his sweep of the Bight but Keyes initially reported them as hostile. It was even harder for the submarines to distinguish friend from foe and one of them was ready to fire before noticing a British ensign. Another *E.6* did actually fire at the *Southampton* which, in turn, attempted to ram the submarine, assuming it to be a German.

The fog caused problems for the Germans, as they were unable to make full use of the coastal batteries on Heligoland. Their other main problem was that it was low water which meant that they were unable to call upon their capital ships as backup because they were behind the Jade bar at the mouth of the Jade. The bar was very difficult for submarines to negotiate and therefore acted as a natural protection, but with the *disadvantage* that they were now facing it. They had at their disposal nine destroyers and nine minesweepers patrolling the Bight, and another minesweeping division, four cruisers, five smaller cruisers and five torpedo-boat flotillas. There were seven cruisers that supported patrols but these were in port and so would take some time to be of any use in the battle.

As the sweep of Heligoland began, the German destroyers dispersed into the mist, limiting the effectiveness of British fire power. Tyrwhitt was having problems with his new flagship as two of her guns failed and she was hit by a German cruiser, restricting her speed capacity. More German cruisers came pouring out of the harbours but the British were lucky. Rather than waiting for his vessels to group together, the German Admiral sent them eagerly forward to try and engage. Nevertheless, as Tyrwhitt began to withdraw from his sweep westwards, the British had not performed as well as they had hoped. Only one German destroyer had been sunk.

Beatty, who was about 40 miles to the north, responded to a request for support from the flotillas, because he was concerned that Goodenough's light cruisers did not have sufficient strength if heavily armed German vessels came out from their nearby bases. It was a risky decision, not simply because of the danger of running into German capital ships, submarines and mines, but because of the poor visibility. However, the support of Goodenough and Beatty proved decisive and, when the British pulled back from the island, they had sunk three German light cruisers. One of them was Admiral Maas's flagship, *Köln*, that went down with the loss of the Admiral. No British ships were lost, although the *Arethusa* and two other destroyers were significantly damaged and had to be towed into port. 35 men were killed to a German death toll of 712. By the time that Admiral Hipper arrived with his battle cruisers, the British had already left.

It was a British victory that was more important in terms of morale than strategy. They had won the first battle of the war and it was in the enemy's home territory. The Kaiser, however, was furious and failed to understand why his entire fleet had not been ordered out when the British were sighted. Hipper made changes in his strategy for the defence of the Bight, deciding that at least four capital ships would be positioned outside the Jade bar in future and that large minefields would be laid to the west of Heligoland. The victory also made the Kaiser, fearful for his High Seas Fleet, even more defensive and he instructed his commander-in-chief that he must have his consent before committing the fleet to action.

The British made another attempt on Heligoland on 11 September but, especially now that highly dangerous minefields had been laid, it was to no avail. The high morale that the British had won started to be eroded as the Germans intensified their submarine warfare. The scout cruiser *Pathfinder* of the Eighth Destroyer Flotilla was torpedoed and sunk by *U.21* in the first successful submarine attack of the war. The British fought back and Lieutenant Commander Max Horton sank the cruiser *Hela* on 13 September and a destroyer on 6 October. However, disaster struck on 22 September when the Germans sank the cruisers *Cressy, Aboukir,* and *Hogue* – three of the six old Bacchantes about which Keyes and Tyrwhitt had been so worried – near the Dutch coast they were patrolling. 62 officers and 1,397 men were lost. The Navy was now just as afraid, if not more so, of the threat from submarines as it was of the High Seas Fleet.

Just as the threat of the submarine had been somewhat underestimated in the British preparations for war, so had the effect of mines. This may have been in part due to the 1907 Hague Convention which ruled against the laying of mines indiscriminately. Minesweepers were a neglected area within the Navy and had little prestige. There were only ten torpedo gunboats and thirteen trawlers that were fitted with sweeps. By the end of the war there would be 726 minesweepers and, by 1917, all vessels were fitted with a parvane that worked by cutting mine moorings. However, at the beginning, none of this was in place.

Jellicoe, believing it to be safer, moved the fleet from anchorage in Loch Ewe to Loch na Keal further south and then to Lough Swilly on the north coast of Ireland. In October, three German minelayers were sent with orders to mine around the Firth of Forth and the River Clyde. Not everything went to plan and the east coast part of the mission had to be aborted. However, the captain of the minelayer *Berlin*, realising that he would not be able to reach the Clyde, instead laid mines off Tory Island, to the northwest of Lough Swilly, although he had no idea that the Grand Fleet was so close by. On 26 October, a merchant vessel fell foul of the mines. The following day, one of the up-to-date superdreadnoughts, the *Audacious*, was out with the Second Battle Squadron on firing exercises. She was hit by a mine. For 12 hours there were frantic efforts to save the ship. The White Star Liner *Olympic* tried to take her in tow but it was all to no avail. Shockingly for the British, the mighty *Audacious* went down, although, until the end of the war, the Admiralty maintained that she had only been damaged. Jellicoe feared that his numeric advantage over the German Fleet was fast disappearing.

British strategy was against laying mines in retaliation, because they wanted to force the German Fleet out of port and engage it rather than hem it in with mines. Another consideration was that mines might impede British traders. There was an additional problem in that, just as minesweepers had been essentially ignored, so had the technology for the mines themselves. It would not be until 1917 that the British were able to produce a mine that operated reliably, and even this was copied from a retrieved German mine.

Despondency was beginning to set in. There was frustration at the lack of opportunity to engage the German Fleet and the general public was wondering what the navy was doing as the German army pushed along the Belgian coast. General Joffre (chief of the French general staff) requested support to protect the ports at Dunkirk and Nieuport. The Germans immediately tried to take advantage by sending vessels to lay mines at the mouth of the Thames on 17 October. The boats were intercepted and sunk, although the success was short-lived and *Hermes*, acting as an aircraft carrier, was lost to a submarine near Calais. This prompted the Admiralty to withdraw any vessels bigger than a destroyer from the Channel east of Greenwich, and to issue an order that such vessels should not cross in the daylight.

28 October saw the return of Jacky Fisher as First Sea Lord, now in his seventies and recalled from retirement. His appointment was a result of the resignation of Prince Louis of Battenberg, mostly because of public ill-feeling about his German birth and family ties. Fisher and Churchill (as First Lord of the Admiralty) were a formidable, volatile and not infallible combination that would ultimately result in them both losing office. Fisher, realising the possibility of a prolonged war, began an ambitious building programme.

The Surface Raiders and the Battles of Coronel and the Falklands

The Surface Raiders

At the beginning of the war, Britain's merchant fleet was by far the largest in the world and Britain was reliant upon her imports, which included two thirds of her food as well as essentials such as iron ore. Such reliance necessarily made Britain vulnerable to attacks on her merchant fleet. The sheer size of the fleet meant that protection for it had to be stretched worldwide. Commerce was an obvious target for the Germans and, later in the war, they would make extensive use of submarines in attacking allied shipping. Over the first six months or so, however, they used surface raiders. The sinking of merchant vessels was not the only aim in striking at commercial shipping. It was also hoped that it would force marine insurance costs so high that they would become prohibitive and halt trade. The British devised a contingency plan for this eventuality before the war, the essence of which was that the government would reinsure 80% of all risks during the war and receive 80% of the premiums. It also meant that merchant vessels were subject to Admiralty directions in respect of all routes and ports of call.

The British efforts to close off exits from the North Sea at the outbreak of war were also part of the plan to protect commercial shipping so that hostile vessels could not reach the main trade routes and only German vessels already stationed abroad could be utilised. In addition, merchant ships were instructed to disperse from their usual routes, so it was clear that there was no intention of protecting them by convoy, the traditional policy. It was felt that, with steam instead of sail, merchantmen had a better chance of fleeing an enemy by taking a route of its own choice, as they did not have to rely on wind directions. In addition, the development of the telegraph made it much more difficult to keep a convoy secret and could give the enemy a chance to prepare an attack. The smoke generated by a large number of ships together would also make them much more visible. The only exception was the use of convoys to protect troopships transporting soldiers from Canada, India, Australia and New Zealand, and this was mostly the result of pressure from the dominion governments. The Admiralty may well have preferred to deploy their ships hunting the German cruisers. In fact, the Germans had very few ships abroad at the start of the war and these were widely scattered in the Atlantic and Pacific. Although the Germans had the second largest merchant marine in the world it was way below the size of the British fleet and they also suffered a major disadvantage in their great lack of overseas bases. This presented a problem in coaling for German vessels, since the regulations of the

1907 Hague Convention limited the amount of coal that could be obtained in a neutral port to that sufficient to allow a ship to reach the nearest port of her own country. Ships were then not allowed to use the same neutral area again for three months.

At the outbreak of war there were two German light cruisers, *Dresden* and *Karlsruhe*, in the West Indies, the light cruiser *Leipzig* was off the American west coast, and the light cruiser *Königsberg* was on the east coast of Africa. In addition there were other minor craft, such as gunboats and survey vessels, which would not really be of any use in an engagement. However the most dangerous force was the heavy-armoured German East Asiatic Squadron, based at Tsingtao, China, under the command of Vice Admiral Count Maximilian von Spee. The squadron was made up of two armoured cruisers, Spee's flagship the *Scharnhorst* and the *Gneisenau*, and the light cruisers *Emden, Leipzig* and *Nürnberg. Scharnhorst* and *Gneisenau* were new sister ships each with eight 8.2 inch and six 5.9 inch guns, and they had won Imperial Navy prizes for their gunnery. The squadron was spread out when the war began. Spee was in the Caroline Islands with *Scharnhorst* and *Gneisenau,* the *Emden* was in Tsingtao and the *Leipzig* was off the Pacific coast of Mexico with *Nürnberg* on her way to relieve her.

The dispersed German force did not appear particularly threatening, especially since Britain and her allies had far larger resources to call upon, including an up-to-date dreadnought, the *Australia*, about 12 armoured cruisers, and some 20 light cruisers. The entry of Japan into the war on 23 August on the side of the Allies significantly increased this power. However, even a lone enemy cruiser could cause havoc by turning up to attack an unsuspecting merchant vessel. In the vast arenas of the Pacific and Atlantic Oceans, it needed a considerably large force to track the enemy down. The British were also nervous about the large number of German merchant vessels that were abroad at the start of the war in neutral ports all over the world; and about the possibility that they could be converted and put to sea, or used as colliers to supply German cruisers. The danger from these potential auxiliary cruisers turned out to be overestimated although some did get through and cause losses to the Allies. These losses might have been much worse if it had not been for their surveillance.

At the outbreak of war Spee recalled *Nürnberg* and headed for the Marianas in the north-western Pacific, where he met with the *Emden* and decided to dispatch her to the Indian Ocean to hamper trade. *Emden* left the base at Tsingtao to avoid being trapped there and, in fact, she might well have been, had the Admiralty not overturned the original war plans of Vice Admiral Sir Martyn Jerram's China Squadron. He was to have been stationed at the mouth of the Yangtze where he would have also been in a position to prevent *Scharnhorst* and *Gneisenau* from returning to Tsingtao from the south. The Admiralty sent him to Hong Kong instead, much to the dismay of Jerram who even considered ignoring the order. Subsequently, forces were sent to cover Jerram's original position but it was a case of shutting the stable door after the horse had bolted. Ultimately, British, Japanese, French and Russian forces would all be employed to hunt down the *Emden*.

Spee wanted to distance himself from Japan, fearing her entry into the war, and sailed with the rest of his squadron eastwards to rendezvous with the *Leipzig* at Easter Island as *Emden* left for her mission. *Emden* was under the command of an exceptionally talented officer, Karl von Müller, and his presence in the Indian Ocean, at the Bay of Bengal (on the Colombo-Calcutta route) came as a total surprise to the Allies who presumed that he was together with Spee and the rest of the squadron. The *Emden* was a modern cruiser, capable of speeds up to 24 knots and had ten 4.1 inch guns and two torpedo tubes. Müller attempted to disguise his ship with a dummy fourth funnel which was only two-dimensional but, from a distance, resembled four-funneled British cruisers. He wasted no time in carrying out his mission and, between 10 and 14 September 1914, he managed to sink six steamers, caught two to serve as colliers and a third to carry captured crews. Normally it would have fallen to Rear Admiral Peirse of the East Indies Station to pursue Muller, but he was occupied with transports from India and the German light cruiser *Königsberg* in the west of the Indian Ocean. Therefore it was the ships *Minotaur, Hampshire* and *Yarmouth* from Jerram's squadron, *Ibuki, Chikuma* and *Yahagi* of the Japanese Navy, *Zhemchug* and *Askold* of the Russian Navy and the French *D'Iberville* that were gathering to pursue *Emden*.

Müller was tenacious and on 22 September he bombarded the Port of Madras, destroying two oil-storage tankers, before sailing to the Minikoi 400 miles west of Colombo, sinking another four ships and taking one other as a collier. Again a sixth was captured and released with crews from the prize vessels. *Emden* then hid futher south at the island of Diego Garcia (so remote that news of the outbreak of war had not yet reached the inhabitants) to attend to repairs and to coal. She had eluded the British, although *Yarmouth* managed to sink one of the German colliers and rescue a Greek ship that had been taken under enemy control. It was not long before Müller was at large again, returning to the Minikoi area and repeating his pattern of sinkings and captures. This time he sank five steamers, retaining one as a collier and releasing another with the crews. Brimming with confidence, Müller headed for Penang and raided the entrance to the Malacca Strait. Using the false funnel, he sank the unsuspecting Russian light cruiser *Zhemtchug* and was about to seize a British steamer carrying explosives when he was distracted by the return of the French destroyer *Mousquet*, which he immediately sank. As a consequence of this latest incident the troop convoys from Australia and New Zealand were delayed so that a more powerful escort could be assembled to protect them. Müller moved on with a mission to raid and destroy the cable and wireless station on Direction Island, and the *Emden* duly arrived on 9 November. A party was sent ashore to sabotage the wireless but, unknown to Müller, the Australian convoy was only 52 miles away, and a warning message had already gone out from the island. The Australian light cruiser *Sydney*, under the command of Captain John Glossop, was sent from the convoy and sailed directly to Direction Island. When the two ships engaged, the *Sydney* had the advantage with her eight 6-inch guns and the *Emden* was run ashore on Keeling Island and burnt out. The landing party had been left behind and managed to escape in a small schooner. They sailed first to Padang where they boarded a German steamer for the Yemen. They then travelled overland, beset by attacks from Bedouins, and did not reach safety in Constantinople until June 1915. In retrospect, the Admiralty felt that convoy protection, despite its inherent problems, would have been a better solution to the threat of the *Emden*.

In the Indian Ocean at the start of the war the Allies were facing a similar threat from the *Königsberg*, a light cruiser with ten 4.1-inch guns, under the command of Captain Looff, based on the East Africa station. Looff's mission was to hinder trade at the entrance to the Red Sea. On 31 July he set sail and managed to avoid a British patrol under the command of Admiral King-Hall, Commander of the Cape Squadron. Unfortunately King-Hall's cruisers were older vessels and their speed capacity could not match the 24 knots of the more modern *Königsberg*. However, the German cruiser was not nearly as successful as the *Emden*, largely because the British hampered her ability to coal. Her collier was kept from leaving port and the British, with some foresight, prevented her from sourcing coal in Portuguese East Africa by buying it up in advance. As a result, only one merchant vessel was sunk before the monsoon season limited the *Königsberg*'s effectiveness even further. She was forced to hide on the African coast, begging coal from any friendly colliers that she encountered. On 20 September, she nevertheless managed to sink an old light cruiser, the *Pegasus*, lowering morale and proving that she was still a threat. On 30 October, the *Dartmouth*, making use of intelligence gathered from a captured supply ship, discovered the *Königsberg* six miles up the Rufgi River. A collier was sunk to block the exit of the river, but the gun range of the British ship could not reach *Königsberg* and, as there were other routes of escape, an expedition had to be organised to finally destroy her. The Royal Naval Air Service attempted to bomb the ship but did not manage to hit her and, in any case, the size of bombs that it was possible for the planes to carry were simply too small. Two monitors, *Mersey* and *Severn*, which were designed for river use, were sent in on 16 July 1915 with aircraft cover and managed to inflict some damage but, although the German ship had been out of action for some time, she was still able to fire and held off the monitors. It took a second attempt on 12 July to finally destroy *Königsberg*. Although ultimately the *Königsberg* did not cause much physical damage, she nevertheless tied up a number of vessels that could have been useful elsewhere and the threat of her presence had also delayed troop convoys from New Zealand.

In the Caribbean, as the war opened, the British were troubled by the presence of the *Karlsruhe,* another new vessel capable of good speed and armed with twelve 4.1 inch guns. In November 1914, the *Karlsruhe* sank as the result of an internal explosion which was a stroke of luck from the Allied perspective but it was not before the German ship had sunk 15 British merchant ships and one Dutch merchant vessel.

The above were the major threats to British shipping, although it is not an exhaustive list. There were other German auxiliary vessels that were able to inflict casualties. However, the most powerful and dangerous German threat was Spee's Squadron.

The Battle of Coronel

After the *Emden* left the squadron, Spee took a course east and, in order to prepare for his arrival in South America, sent the *Nürnberg* on to Honolulu with instructions for German agents in South America to arrange coal and provisions. When the Japanese declared war there was, of course, no possibility of a return to Tsingtao. On 30 September, he arrived at Papeete in Tahiti and shelled French installations and, in addition, sank a gunboat before feinting a course northeast.

On 4 October Spee was being hunted by British, Australian, New Zealand, French and Japanese forces and a clue was now given to his whereabouts. An Allied ship picked up a wireless message from the *Scharnhorst*, indicating a course for Marquesas and Easter Island. Accordingly, the Allied forces were rearranged.

One of the strongest British squadrons in the hunt was from the South American Station under the command of the popular Rear-Admiral Sir Christopher Cradock, whose responsibility was to guard the Magellan Straits. Cradock's base was the Falkland Islands where he had two armoured cruisers, *Good Hope* and *Monmouth*, both of which were over ten years old and had a design fault in that their casemates were so close to the waterline that they often could not be fired. Even when they could be fired, their capacity was only about 50 per cent of the capacity of the German cruisers. In addition to these problems, the majority of his crews were reservists who had not been together very long and lacked gunnery practice. As well as the armoured cruisers, Cradock had one modern light cruiser, *Glasgow*, and a converted liner, *Otranto*, with some 4.7-inch guns.

Cradock was to keep his force ready to engage *Scharnhorst* and *Gneisenau* and he was promised reinforcements in the shape of the battleship *Canopus* and the cruiser *Defence* from the Mediterranean. The intended reinforcement, *Defence*, was equal to one of Spee's cruisers but the rest of Cradock's squadron would still have been at a disadvantage. However, it was decided that *Defence* would be better deployed with a cruiser squadron operating further north in the Atlantic. Finally, she would be ordered to join Cradock, although she would not arrive until the battle had been fought. This left the *Canopus*, a battleship with 12-inch guns. Spee's ships were much faster than *Canopus* and, although Spee was not to know it, his smaller guns could, in fact, outrange those on the

British ship. Once Cradock had the superior force, he was to search the straits, though he was also to be prepared either to come back to cover the River Plate or to search as far as Valparaiso, depending upon intelligence received. His mission was to hamper German trade as well as to destroy the German cruisers.

On 18 October 1914, Spee sailed from Easter Island, where he had coaled, to Mas-a-Fuera which was more remote and halfway to the Chilean coast. He now had three light cruisers in his company in addition to his armoured vessels. Cradock, at Port Stanley, heard on the same day that the arrival of *Canopus* would be delayed by a week, and that her speed capacity was not the 15 knots that he was expecting but about 12, which would slow down his squadron. Once she arrived, he left Port Stanley and headed through the Magellan Straits and up the west coast of Chile. *Canopus* followed behind, convoying the colliers.

At the same time *Glasgow* had been on the lookout for Spee and was heading for the port of Coronel on the Chilean coast to rendezvous with Cradock. German intelligence picked up on these movements on 31 October and Spee hoped to intercept the British force which he trusted would be inferior to his own. Late on the afternoon of 1 November, he found *Glasgow*, along with *Good Hope*, *Monmouth* and *Otranto*. Cradock had been hoping to intercept *Leipzig* and he knew her to be in the area from wireless signals. This had been intended by Spee all along and he had only transmitted from *Leipzig* in order to hide the presence of the other cruisers.

At around 5pm the *Glasgow* spotted Spee's squadron and Cradock prepared for battle, lining up the *Good Hope, Monmouth, Glasgow* and *Otranto*. He turned course towards the German ships – *Scharnhorst, Gneisenau, Leipzig* and *Dresden* (the *Nürnberg* would join later) – with the intention of immediate engagement while the Germans had the sun directly in their vision. However, Spee would not be drawn in. Before the battle started, Cradock realised that the *Otranto* would be very vulnerable and of little practical use and sent her away to safety.

The Germans waited until just before 7pm when visibility for the British was at its worst – as the sun set they were silhouetted in failing light and it was increasingly difficult to have a clear sight of the German vessels in the dusk. The expert German gunnery quickly overwhelmed *Good Hope* and *Monmouth* which were both sunk with the loss of all hands. It was only 8.20am when the *Glasgow* had to abandon *Monmouth*, as nothing could be done, and attempt to warn the approaching *Canopus*, hampered by the Germans jamming wireless transmissions until *Glasgow* was out of range. It was the first time that the Royal Navy had been defeated at sea in over 100 years. It was a huge shock to the system.

The Battle of the Falklands

On 4 November, Fisher, who had been back in office for only five days, heard of the disaster and immediately ordered the two battle cruisers, *Invincible* and *Inflexible*, to the South Atlantic. They were fitted in record time and placed under the command of Vice Admiral Sturdee, who was chosen largely because Fisher, blaming him for what he considered the poor deployment of ships, wanted him out of his position as Chief of Staff at the Admiralty. The deployment was a risk as it undermined Jellicoe's margin of superiority in this class of battleship against that of the High Seas Fleet in the North Sea. Jellicoe was understandably anxious but Fisher was bold in taking the risk and, in addition, the *Princess Royal*, another battle cruiser, was dispatched to North American waters. However, the biggest question was where Spee would plan to go next. There were many options and the Allies had to try to second guess them all.

The fear was that Spee would take a course through the Panama Canal into the Caribbean and overwhelm the small Allied force in the West Indies. Should he accomplish this, then he would be free to proceed to New York and release the considerable numbers of German liners trapped there, protected only by Admiral Hornby's elderly squadron. There were also whispers that a German battle cruiser might escape to attack North Atlantic sea routes and operate in conjunction with Spee off the Plate, if Spee's course turned out to be around Cape Horn.

Admiral Hornby took his force to the West Indies to prevent Spee entering the Panama Canal and the *Princess Royal* was deployed in Jamaica. Also in South America was Admiral Stoddart's force, comprising the armoured cruisers *Carnarvon, Cornwall, Defence, Canopus, Kent, Glasgow, and Otranto* (some of which had been redeployed from Cradock's squadron), which was to wait at Montevideo, later changed to Abrolhos Rocks, for Sturdee to join them.

If Spee went round the Horn the worry was that he would head for South Africa and stir up anti-British feeling. Before the Battle of Coronel an old battleship, the *Albion*, was sent to the Cape Station to join Admiral King-Hall and his two small cruisers, *Hyacinth* and *Astraea*. They were subsequently joined by the light cruiser *Weymouth* and by the armoured cruisers *Minotaur* and *Defence* so that the force would be sufficient to combat Spee. On the West African coast, to counteract any German action against British and French colonies, a new squadron was temporarily put together by deploying vessels from the Mediterranean and the Channel. In the Pacific, the British and Japanese worked together to combat Spee and to prevent him from trying to double back and head for the Indian Ocean.

On 7 December 1914 *Invincible* and *Inflexible*, after a short delay, reached Port Stanley in the Falkland Islands and Admirals Sturdee and Stoddart made their rendezvous. As the British ships were coaling, *Gneisenau* and *Nürnberg* approached Port William, north of Stanley, unseen other than by *Canopus* which opened fire on them at about 9am. Coaling stopped abruptly and the ships made ready to sail. The German cruisers made a dash to join Spee in the *Scharnhorst* but this proved to be a tactical error. If Spee had moved towards the cruisers, he could have blocked the British, preventing them from leaving port and attacking them there. However, Spee had not received the intelligence from Germany that British cruisers were in the area. Now his ships were under serious threat from the strengthened British force. They hoped to evade the British during the night but were under fire by 1pm. Spee hoped that he could save his light cruisers and, splitting his squadron, he sent them off, facing the fire with just *Scharnhorst* and *Gneisenau*.

There was some doubt as to whether *Invincible* and *Inflexible* would fulfil their potential, since their shooting appeared poor to the other British ships, especially in comparison to Spee's crack gunnery, and their vision was impaired by the amount of smoke throughout the action. Sturdee was endeavouring to keep out of range of the German 8.2-inch guns but within his own range of 12-inch guns and he managed this with great prowess. Spee attempted to make a dash towards bad weather but the British were in full pursuit and there was only a temporary ceasefire. Sturdee closed range and soon overwhelmed *Scharnhorst*. Fire spread through her and, at 4.15pm, she went down with the loss of all hands. The *Gneisenau* fought bravely on but she too was overwhelmed and sank at 6pm although some 200 of her crew were rescued. By coincidence, one of the German lieutenants rescued by the *Carnarvon* was named Stoddart and turned out to be a German relation of the British admiral.

Sturdee had also divided his ships at the beginning of the battle and sent some in pursuit of Spee's dispatched light cruisers. *Cornwall* and *Glasgow* chased the *Leipzig* while *Kent* followed *Nürnberg*. It looked as if *Nürnberg* would outrun her pursuer but, under pressure, two of her boilers blew and *Kent* closed in to fire and sunk her. The battle for *Leipzig* went on for two hours and she fired three torpedoes at the British ships, though none found their target, before she succumbed and sank. The only German vessel to escape was the *Dresden* which did manage to outrun *Carnarvon*. However, she was hunted down three months later, hiding in the Juan Fernandez Islands. *Kent* and *Glasgow* opened fire and *Dresden* scuttled, since she was out of coal, largely because the British had been jamming her radio so that she could not rendezvous with her collier.

The Battle of the Falklands was the most decisive battle of the war so far, and important in terms of the Allies' morale as well as for Atlantic and Pacific trade. There were, of course, still things to be learnt and the pursuit of Spee highlighted the problems with British gunnery that would continue for the duration of the war. The hit rate at the Battle of the Falklands was 5%, which, although it would become an acceptable standard later, was not considered a good average at the time. Gunnery training before the war had failed to simulate battle conditions sufficiently and smoke was a constant hindrance to vision, not simply from coal-fired guns but also, depending on the weather conditions, from the funnels. There were additional problems in that direct fire-controllers had not been installed, and the nearest supply of 12-inch shell was miles away in Gibraltar. Also as a result of the Falklands success, Fisher ordered two new battle cruisers, *Repulse* and

Renown, as well as three of what he called large light cruisers, named *Courageous, Glorious* and *Furious*, which were almost the same thing.

Dogger Bank

Back at the Admiralty, the Allies had been lucky in the recovery of a German Navy cipher signal book from a cruiser that was destroyed by the Russians in the Gulf of Finland. In addition, they also picked up confidential charts of the North Sea, showing the German operational grid to locate friendly and enemy vessels, after they were abandoned as a German destroyer sank. So that full advantage could be made of this intelligence a top-secret department was created within the Admiralty, which became known as 'Room 40'. The men in Room 40 were able to decipher German messages and, although the enemy quickly realised this, they thought that they could counteract it by continually changing codes. The British, however, were able to keep up with the changes. German intelligence could probably have taken advantage of the British in the same way but for the fact that the Royal Navy, unlike the Germans who used them without restriction, made rather limited use of radio transmissions.

Admiral Franz von Hipper had begun raids at the beginning of November, with some successes in mine laying and the destruction of smaller vessels, when Room 40 was not yet in existence. On 24 January 1915, he went out with the intention of attacking British ships near the important fishing ground of Dogger Bank. He hoped to find fishing trawlers and he also had intelligence that suggested there were some light naval vessels without protection in the area. This time the Admiralty was able to inform Beatty that Hipper was at large, and Beatty set off with five battle cruisers, hoping to intercept the Germans unawares.

Hipper had hoped that he might be able to secure the support of the High Seas Fleet if they ventured out to the eastern part of the North Sea but the Kaiser was committed to his policy of caution and refused. Admiral Ingenohl, who had led raids on the east coast of England therefore allocated the First and Second scouting groups. These comprised of battle cruisers, four light cruisers and two flotillas of torpedo boats. Hipper had two battle cruisers, *Moltke* and *Derfflinger*, and a rather slow armoured cruiser, *Blücher*. Ingenohl was unaware of course that the Admiralty was aware of his intentions and that the Royal Navy intended to set a trap. Beatty and his battle cruisers would be joined by Goodenough's light cruiser squadron, the Harwich force under Tyrwhitt with three light cruisers and thirty-five destroyers, and Keyes with the destroyers *Lurcher* and *Firedrake*. British submarines were sent towards Borkum Riff, off the German coast. The Third Battle Squadron and the Third Cruiser Squadron were sent to patrol to the north should the Germans attempt to escape that way, and to their north Jellicoe sailed out of Scapa Flow to make a sweep in case the High Seas Fleet came out.

At dawn on 24 December, light cruiser *Aurora* went into action with the cruiser *Kolberg* and both Beatty and Hipper headed towards them. Hipper realised from intercepting radio messages that the British might well be out in force which meant that he could be heading into a trap. He therefore changed course and headed towards German waters. Beatty had already sighted his ships and gave chase. Just after 9am he had closed the gap sufficiently to open fire with *Lion, Tiger* and *Princess Royal*. The slower battle cruisers *New Zealand* and *Indomitable* were coming up to the rear. Hipper faced them with *Seydlitz* in front and *Moltke, Derfflinger* and *Blucher* following.

It should have been a resounding British victory, but there were problems with signalling due to poor visibility and some serious damage from German firing to the *Lion* which disabled her. *Tiger* misinterpreted a message from Beatty and consequently left *Moltke* unengaged and free to attack the British frontline. *Blücher* was soon overcome, *Seydlitz* lost two turrets with one hit and both *Derfflinger* and *Kolberg* sustained heavy damage. *Lion* was hit by three German shells and, as she began to fall astern, command had to pass from Beatty to Rear Admiral Moore. As *Lion* had no electricity, Beatty could no longer send wireless messages and his signal halyards were damaged which made signalling difficult and disastrously confusing. Moore believed that Beatty intended him to attack the rear of the enemy rather than giving chase to the German front-runners, so he concentrated on the already damaged *Blücher*. The signal that Beatty had wanted to send was 'engage the enemy more closely', just as Nelson had done at Trafalgar, but he was frustrated and furious to find that it was no longer in the signal book. Even so, *Moltke* was the only German vessel that was in a position to fight and she drew back, thinking that she had sunk *Tiger*. Tyrwhitt arrived with a light cruiser and four destroyers and concentrated fire on the *Blücher*, along with *Tiger* who had brought her fires under control. *Blücher* was duly sunk with unnecessary British force, and 234 of her 1,200 crew were rescued – it would have been more if a German zeppelin had not begun to bomb the British ships picking up the sailors, assuming that they were rescuing their own. By the time that Beatty had moved to the destroyer *Attack* and reached *Princess Royal* to board, the rest of the Germans had got away despite the heavy damage that the ships had taken.

It was a British victory but a disappointing one. As a result of the poor choices he had made, Moore was deployed to command an old squadron of cruisers based in the Canary Islands where there was less chance of major action. It was more serious for the Germans who had drawn some consolation from thinking that they had sunk the *Tiger*. When this turned out to be false, it was decided that Von Pohl should replace the commander-in-chief Ingenohl.

Strategy changes took place on both sides. Tirpitz, despite having largely been responsible for the building of the dreadnoughts on the German side, now favoured airship attacks on London and submarine attacks on British trade. The British abandoned the regular cruising of their more powerful ships hoping to take German vessels by chance at the beginning of 1915, and later the same year this was also considered an ineffective strategy to be undertaken by lighter vessels. The increasing threat from submarines made it too dangerous to take such chances and, in future, vessels would only go out for specific purposes – offensive operations, exercises and to respond to intelligence reports on enemy operations. For both sides a decisive strike remained elusive.

Turkey and Mesopotamia

Germany and Turkey 1914

Before the war Britain had been keen to maintain good relations with Turkey, since it was strategically important in terms of access to the Black Sea and communications with Russia. In 1908, power in Turkey had been taken by a group of young officers who wanted to modernize the country and this attracted considerable German investment in infrastructure and in training the army. Britain, meanwhile, was working with the Turkish navy, and British yards were building two brand new dreadnoughts for them. The ships were ready for delivery in August 1914. Churchill, on the brink of war, made an order that they should be compulsorily transferred to the British Fleet, which naturally outraged the Turks. They were not pacified by an offer from the Admiralty to pay a fixed daily rate for the use of the ships for the duration of the war.

The British deployment in the Mediterranean was quite small at the beginning of the war, as most of the Fleet had been concentrated in the North Sea, and it was expected that France would take most of the responsibility for the area. Historically, this was a big turnaround in British naval policy, although, as the war went on, events forced them to deploy more resources in this arena. The French had a powerful battleship force at Toulon although only one dreadnought. However, the Commander-in-Chief of the Mediterranean, Admiral Sir Archibald Milne, had at his disposal the 2nd Battle Cruiser Squadron, Rear Admiral Troubridge's 1st Cruiser Squadron as well as four light cruisers and a flotilla of 16 destroyers. Many thought that Milne was in command more because of his connections in society than because of his naval prowess. In the days leading up to Britain's entry into the war, Milne was given orders that his first priority was to assist the French in transporting their African army from Algeria over to France, all the more necessary as the French had sent two of her most modern dreadnoughts to escort the president on a state trip to Russia. According to his orders, Milne was also, if possible, to bring 'to action individual fast German ships, particularly the *Goeben*, who may interfere with that transportation... Do not at this stage be brought to action against superior forces, except in combination with the French as part of a general battle.' In fairness to Milne, it was, in light of what transpired, a rather unclear message, but it was even more unfortunate that it should have been sent to an admiral not renowned for his intellect or initiative.

The Germans had only two vessels in the Mediterranean, the aforementioned *Goeben*, a battle cruiser, and a fast modern light cruiser, the *Breslau*, under the command of Admiral Souchon. There were other potential enemies in the shape of a small Austro-Hungarian force and a larger Italian one, although on 2 August Italy declared neutrality. However, the biggest threats to the French transports remained the German vessels.

On 3 August, British intelligence learned that Souchon's ships were coaling at Messina in Sicily. The Admiralty presumed that they would now head west and the fear was that they would escape the Mediterranean through the Straits of Gibraltar and be a potential menace to British Atlantic trade vessels. Accordingly, Milne ordered two battle cruisers that were watching the entrance to the Adriatic (in case Souchon should attempt to meet up with the Austro-Hungarian fleet) to sail at high speed to Gibraltar with the intention of intercepting the *Goeben*.

Although Souchon did sail west he was, in fact, heading for Africa where, on 4 August, he bombarded the French ports of Bone and Philippeville. There was not much damage but the incident caught the French off guard. As the *Goeben* and *Breslau* headed back east they met the British battle cruisers, *Indomitable* and *Inflexible*, that had been sent to intercept them. Technically, Britain and Germany were not yet at war, as the British ultimatum did not expire until midnight. As a result, the two groups of ships sailed past in opposite directions without acknowledging each other. The British cruisers switched course in order to shadow the Germans and were joined by *Dublin*, a light cruiser. When Souchon went ahead on full speed it became a stern chase. The British were outrun and Souchon returned to

Messina. When Milne heard of Souchon's location, he again presumed that the eventual destination would be west either to the Adriatic or to pass through to the Atlantic. The Admiralty ordered him to patrol the Adriatic to prevent the Germans entering or the Austrians from leaving without being seen. Accordingly, Milne sent heavy ships between Sicily and Tunisia in the hope of intercepting the *Goeben* and Troubridge was sent with four armoured cruisers to the entrance to the Adriatic. Although the French had ample protection from their own Toulon squadrons, the Admiralty had not sent word of this to Milne and so his order to protect the transports was still valid.

On 6 August, the light cruiser *Gloucester* sighted the German ships leaving Messina through the Straits. Only *Gloucester* followed through the straits – although a more belligerent admiral might have done so, Milne did not send more heavily armed craft in order to respect Italian neutrality. Captain Howard Kelly of the *Gloucester* sent messages to Troubridge, who was patrolling south of Corfu, and to Milne, who was well to the west, that Souchon appeared to be heading for the Adriatic. He sent further word when Souchon changed course to the south and the *Breslau* split away – this was confirmed by the *Dublin* (captained by Kelly's brother John) which had intercepted Souchon's wireless communications while on the way to join Troubridge with two destroyers. Souchon was, in fact, heading for Constantinople where a friendly agreement with Germany had been signed and where he would have free entry. The course towards the Adriatic had been a feint but Troubridge, believing the new course was the feint, continued with his course to Corfu, thinking that he could engage Souchon there.

Gloucester kept close to *Goeben* and was instructed to signal the position to *Dublin*. Possibly *Dublin* would have been able to intercept but the ships slipped past each other in the darkness. Troubridge maintained his passage north until midnight, even though Milne could have told him by 10.30pm that the *Goeben* was definitely pursuing a southward course. Early in the morning, Breslau was seen to have rejoined *Goeben*, and the *Gloucester* joined *Dublin* as they shadowed the German vessels. Troubridge signalled that he was on his way to support them. In the meantime, his gunnery expert convinced Troubridge that he was putting his four cruisers under too great a risk – that the ten 11-inch and ten 6-inch guns of the *Goeben* would destroy the cruisers before they could get into range with their own twenty-two 9.2-inch, fourteen 7.5-inch, and sixteen 6-inch guns. Troubridge went against his own instincts and decided not to give chase.

Milne could have sent *Indomitable* but instead decided to refuel with his entire squadron at Malta and then spent needless time on a course for the Adriatic in response to an erroneous Admiralty signal that said that Austria had declared war on Britain six days before this was the case. *Gloucester* and *Dublin* were still in pursuit of Souchon and *Gloucester* managed to engage the *Breslau* but was obliged to pull back as she had no more coal. *Dublin* informed Milne that Souchon's intended destination was Constantinople, having intercepted the message, but Milne, now believing that Austria had declared war, continued to hold back, thinking that Souchon might still turn back if Austria also declared war on Italy. The German vessels escaped and made their way up the Dardanelles to Constantinople.

The implications of the catalogue of mistakes and failures to intercept the vessels soon became apparent. *Breslau* and *Goeben* were presented to the Turkish Navy, becoming the *Midilli* and *Selim* respectively. Germans replaced the British naval mission officers on board Turkish ships and, under pressure from Germany, Turkey declared war on the German side. In addition to the undermining of British esteem, all this ultimately led to the Dardanelles campaign and was responsible for isolating Russia. Fisher was furious, seeing it as a shameful incident, and he blamed Milne of whom he had never thought highly. An inquiry by the Admiralty decided that Troubridge had had 'a very fair chance of at least delaying *Goeben* by materially damaging her'. Therefore, there had to be a court martial, and Troubridge was charged that he did 'from negligence or through other default, forbear to pursue the chase of His Imperial German Majesty's ship *Goeben*, then flying'. Some even felt that he should have been tried on the higher charge of cowardice but he was eventually cleared on the grounds that he was following Admiralty orders, such as they were, as transmitted through Milne. It exposed the inefficiency of the staff work at the Admiralty as well as Milne's lack of judgement. Though acquitted, Troubridge was not employed at sea again and was given land-based commands that fell below his expectations. Milne also never served at sea again and saw out the war on half pay.

Forcing the Dardanelles

For some months after the incident with *Goeben* and *Breslau*, Britain hoped to be able to keep Turkey neutral and, at the end of August, Greece had even offered her forces with a plan to land troops on the Gallipoli peninsula with the aim of giving the Allies control of the Dardanelles. In order not to antagonise Turkey, the offer had been turned down. However, at the end of October, a Turkish squadron, working with Souchon, bombarded Russian ports in the Black Sea. On 31 October Britain declared war on Turkey. Vice Admiral Sackville Hamilton Carden's Dardanelles Squadron was ordered by Churchill to bombard the forts on the Gallipoli coast in early November. The bombardments of the forts were effective to some extent but they were not followed up and so the main consequence was to draw attention to the importance of the region to the Allies and to highlight the threat of attack to the Germans and Turks. There were several reasons why Britain was interested in control of this area. Most importantly, the Gallipoli peninsula divided the Aegean Sea from the Dardanelles and the approach to the Turkish capital, then Constantinople, on the Sea of Marmara, and beyond that to the Black Sea which bordered Russia. If a successful campaign could be mounted, it was hoped that it would relieve pressure on the

Army on the Western Front as well as pressure on Russia, since Germany would have to divert resources to the area. It was also hoped that this would ultimately shorten the war and break the deadlock on the Western Front. Britain was also concerned by the threat that the Turkish army (her Navy was very small) posed to the Suez Canal, the crucial route to the Middle East and India. Indeed, on 3 February 1915, the Turks mounted an attack on the canal from the Sinai Desert. They failed but remained in Sinai until they were forced out in 1916, thus requiring a large deployment of Allied vessels, along with troops from Britain and India, to protect the canal. The southern approaches were also protected with ships in the Gulf of Suez, the Red Sea and the Gulf of Aqaba. It tied up a lot of vessels that would have been useful in the Dardanelles.

There was much discussion about how to deal with the situation in Turkey. Churchill was an enthusiastic advocate for an operation to force the Dardanelles including action ashore on Gallipoli, and he was largely responsible for the disastrous campaign to come. Fisher, foreseeing many problems, was set against it and worried about deploying vessels away from the Grand Fleet. Churchill won through and a base was established at the Greek Island of Lemnos in the Aegean Sea. Churchill conceived it primarily as a naval campaign, although there were also plans to land troops. Fisher thought that it should be an amphibious affair if it was to go ahead and the commander-in-chief of the Mediterranean Fleet, Admiral Limpus, argued that the army should deal with the forts rather than fire from the ships. However, the Australian and New Zealand Army Corps based in Egypt were put on alert to move to Lemnos, and the British 29th Division was initially on standby, although this was overturned by Kitchener. He did not agree to release the division until 10 March, by which time it would be too late for them to participate in the naval attack.

It was intended that land forces would take control of the forts along the coast so that the naval vessels could pass freely into the Dardanelles and move on to take Constantinople. It was not an easy exercise because there were 14 forts in total and six of these surrounded the Narrows, a bottleneck in the waters that was less than a mile wide. They were all armed with guns ranging between 4 and 14 inches and, although some of them were outdated, they were nevertheless operational and a threat to the ships. In between the forts, batteries of howitzers had been installed and there was a constant threat of mines in the water. In addition to this, the Dardanelles were difficult to navigate anyway. Never more than three miles wide with strong currents and many shallows, they were particularly difficult for submarine manoeuvres. Converted trawlers were requisitioned to clear the mines which prevented the battleships getting close enough to the forts to disable them. The trawlers, however, could not really be effective while they were under threat from the guns and howitzers, and the strong currents made it impossible for them to move at a speed of more than three knots.

The plan was that the Dardanelles Squadron would blast

the forts at the outer areas and, if necessary, land forces to complete the demolition. Then the minesweepers would neutralise the minefields so that the ships could get in range of the forts around the Narrows. Once this was accomplished, the Allies would gain passage into the Sea of Marmara and then launch a major naval attack to force the Turks into surrender at Constantinople. On 19 February 1915, Admiral Carden began bombardments at Sedd-el-Bahr and Kum Kale, with the pre-dreadnoughts *Agamemnon, Vengeance, Triumph* and *Cornwallis*, the battle cruiser *Inflexible* and the cruiser *Amethyst*. There were additional destroyers as well as three French battleships, *Bouvet, Gaulois* and *Suffren*. They made a second attempt on 25 February since, despite the heavy bombardment, little impact had been made on the forts, and there was some damage to ships as well as casualties from the Turkish guns. The second bombardment was more successful and this time marines and sailors were landed the following day to disable any remaining guns.

In the meantime, *Ark Royal* had reached Lemnos, carrying six aircraft that would be used for reconnaissance and provide the fleet with feedback on where shells fell. Some submarine commanders accompanied pilots on reconnaissance trips so that they were able to locate minefields as well as potential targets. It was one of the first attempts at using planes for observation and, due to unreliable equipment and the novice observers, it was not altogether successful.

From 1 March onwards bombardments took place

virtually every day and reinforcements, in the form of the battleship *Swiftsure* and the ultra-modern *Queen Elizabeth*, were deployed to the squadron. At first, the landing parties received little attention on shore but they were increasingly subject to resistance. Although they managed to disable the guns, the Turks were able to get them functioning again fairly quickly and, since the troops were picked up again after each mission, they found it impossible to take command of the forts. It was also a frustrating job for the minesweepers. When they were able to get through, under covering fire from the battleships, they were continually forced to retreat by the howitzer fire. Carden resigned under great stress, close to a breakdown, and was replaced by Vice Admiral John de Robeck. The Dardanelles were proving more difficult to break through than had been anticipated and, more than ever, military assistance looked necessary. However, arrangements for the Mediterranean Expeditionary Force that was slowly gathering at Lemnos were disorganised and beset with logistic problems, which ultimately meant that many of the troops would not be ready before the naval attack.

The major attack under de Robeck was made on 18 March, with British and French ships attempting to force the straits, essentially in three lines. In the first line were *Queen Elizabeth, Agamemnon, Lord Nelson* and *Inflexible*. The French made up the second line, commanded by their Admiral Guepratte, with *Charlemagne, Bouvet, Gaulois,* and *Suffren*. The third comprised the British ships *Albion, Irresistible, Ocean* and *Vengeance*. Flanking the ships on the

Gallipoli shore were *Majestic* and *Prince George* and on the Asiatic side were *Triumph* and *Swiftsure*. The plan was to silence the fort guns and then send in the minesweepers. The firing went on from just after 11am until 4pm. The guns from the outer forts and on the Narrows were successfully silenced, but the ships were unable to deal with the Turkish artillery and the mobile batteries, making it impossible for the minesweepers to get through. The French ship *Bouvet* struck a mine. There was a huge explosion as her magazine blew and she sank very quickly with the loss of the majority of her crew. The trawlers kept on trying to make it through to clear the mines but they were incessantly fired at by the howitzers and, in the end, they had to withdraw. Just after 4pm *Inflexible* struck a mine and, although she was not sunk, she would be out of action for over a month. *Irresistible* hit a mine and, when *Ocean* went to her assistance, she met the same fate. *Irresistible* foundered that night. De Robeck called off the operation.

In fact, the Turks were almost out of ammunition when the Allies retreated and it was the minefields that had saved them. (Apart from the mines that had found targets, they were all still in place, making the Dardanelles as difficult as ever for the Allies to penetrate.) At the end of the day, the sustained bombardment had only knocked out a few guns. One of the main reasons for attempting to force the Dardanelles had, of course, been to relieve the pressure on Russia but, elsewhere, the crisis in the Caucasus proved an overwhelming victory for the Russians against the Turks. What was demoralising for other Allied troops was that the

Russian success had been won before the bombardment had started but they had not been informed.

That night Admiral Roger Keyes arrived in the destroyer *Jed*. He had been transferred from the Harwich submarine command to de Robeck's chief of staff, to see if the pre-dreadnoughts could be saved. He found them both sunk. Believing that the Turkish forts had been overcome, he was all for de Robeck trying again and he began to reorganise the minesweepers and to fit destroyers with sweeping equipment which would be able to work better under fire. It was a pity that this had not been thought of before the attack. De Robeck refused to go in again, unless it was a combined operation – probably a sensible decision since the Turkish forts had sustained only minor losses. A conference of the leaders, both military and naval, took place on board the *Queen Elizabeth* and it was decided that a joint operation should take place in April.

De Robeck's refusal to try again without the Army was made despite the fact that Churchill was in favour of another naval effort. Fisher and other colleagues also opposed Churchill and were becoming increasingly disgruntled with him. As usual Fisher, with Jellicoe and Beatty behind him, was worried about further resources being taken from the Grand Fleet. He believed that, because of the pressure that Germany was placing on Holland to enter the war on her side, there would soon be action in the North Sea. In the meantime, the British battleships in the Gallipoli area were still in danger. The Germans seriously upgraded the defences and the Turkish deployed more troops. The Germans also decided to send submarines to the Mediterranean and a pair of submarines by rail to Turkish waters that would be assembled on arrival. These were a threat but they were not there in time for the landings on the Gallipoli peninsula which took place on 25 April.

In the lead up to the campaign, the port of Murdos at Lemnos was transformed into a harbour and jetties and pontoons installed. Altogether 75,000 troops had been assembled by General Hamilton. The British 29th Division was landed at the tip of the Peninsula at Cape Helles, and the ANZACs (Australian and New Zealand Army Corps) landed further north to establish a beachhead. French forces were placed on the Asiatic side to create a diversion. The Turkish forces could not force the troops back into the sea but neither could the Allies push past them, even with more reinforcements, to get to the commanding height of Achi Baba. The situation rapidly deteriorated into a stale-mate.

The Navy had a logistic nightmare on their hands in supplying the army, giving artillery support and preparing for the imminent submarine arrivals reported by intelli-gence. The Navy had itself been successful in getting submarines into the Sea of Marmara despite the difficulty of navigating the Dardanelles.

Then, on 13 May, a Turkish destroyer with a German crew torpedoed and sunk *Goliath* with the loss of all hands. As a result, Fisher was adamant that the super-dreadnought *Queen Elizabeth* should return with immediate effect and threatened to resign over the issue. (He had already threatened to resign at least seven times in 1915.) Churchill conceded but only on the condition that *Queen Elizabeth* was replaced with two pre-dreadnoughts and two monitors. This was not the end of the wrangling in the War Council over deployments and reinforcements in the Dardanelles. It was a depressing point in the war anyway. A new offensive on the Western Front was already going badly and there was a chronic lack of shells. On 14 May, at the War Council meeting, Churchill and Fisher agreed the naval reinforcements for the Dardanelles, although Fisher was not entirely satisfied since they included vessels that he had been allowed to build for his Baltic project. Overnight, however, Churchill substantially revised what had been agreed, demanding even more, and, not for the first time, sent a memorandum that Fisher found patronising in tone. It was the final straw and Fisher really did walk out of the Admiralty on 15 May. There was a huge outcry with everybody, from the Queen to the newspapers, appealing for him to stay. He then wrote to Prime Minister Asquith to withdraw the resignation but he made a number of ill-judged conditions – that Churchill be removed both from office and the cabinet, that there should be a completely new board of Admiralty, that Churchill's successor should deal only with policy and parliamentary procedure, that Fisher himself should have sole responsibility for all new shipbuilding and that he should have complete professional charge of the war at sea. In the meantime he had refused to carry out any duties at the Admiralty even though Room

40 had decoded intelligence that indicated that the High
Seas Fleet was possibly coming out. There were questions
over his sanity and his supporters fell away. His resignation
was officially accepted on 22 May. The whole affair also
brought much pressure to bear on Churchill and he was
also forced to give his resignation in May. The extraordi-
nary partnership was broken. The Dardanelles incident and
the aftermath may have warranted their dismissal but it
should not be forgotten that both had been instrumental
and beneficial in preparing the navy for war.

Just as Churchill was forced out of office on 25 May, the
German submarines arrived in the Dardanelles. Although
de Robeck received a warning of the presence of *U-21* and
took precautions by limiting ship movements and
protecting them with anti-torpedo nets, the submarine
torpedoed and sunk the battleship *Triumph* and, on the 27
May, the battleship *Majestic* met the same fate. On a
second mission in July, the submarine took the French
steamer *Carthage*. Despite this good start, the British
defences were reasonably effective and so German
submarines did not prove decisive in the Dardanelles. The
British submarine offensive was one of the most successful
parts of the Dardanelles campaign, taking over 200 vessels
including a battleship, and they operated in the Sea of
Marmara from April until the completion of the
Dardanelles campaign. Overall, however, there was still a
deadlock.

A renewed effort was mounted by Hamilton who
landed a further 22,000 troops at Suvla Bay, starting on 8

August. From a naval point of view, the landings went well. The Army, however, having caught the Turks unawares, failed to capitalise on their advantage and did not push forward quickly enough under Lieutenant General Stopford who rested the troops for a day. The Oglue Tepe, an important strongpoint, was unoccupied when the Allies arrived at Sulva but, by the time they advanced, the Turks had organised their troops and the Allies lost over 8,000 men. The French too were determined to break the stalemate and planned to open up a second front at Yukyeri on the Asiatic side of the peninsula by deploying another four divisions from France. However, they never got that far. When Bulgaria entered the war on the side of the Germans they were diverted, together with British troops, to Salonika in what turned out to be a wasted effort to march north to try and save Serbia.

With Bulgaria in the war and with commitments to a new front in Macedonia, in addition to the overall lack of progress, the huge number of fatalities and the sickness among the troops in the Dardanelles, evacuation was really the only option remaining. The ever buoyant Keyes still pressed for a final naval attack but de Robeck remained unconvinced. There was some support from Kitchener, and also from the French. There were fears that, because the landings themselves had resulted in a high number of casualties, the evacuation might cause even higher numbers. The ultimate decision, made in December, was for evacuation. Another factor governing this decision was that a direct rail link between Germany and Constantinople was about to be opened which would give the Turks a constant munitions supply.

The evacuation was one of the most well organised aspects of the Gallipoli and Dardanelles campaign, and did not result in the anticipated heavy losses of human life. It had to take place secretly under the cover of darkness so as not to provoke a Turkish attack. The Royal Navy had to arrange the transport of 118,000 men, 7,000 horses and mules as well as artillery from Anzac Cove, Helles and Suvla. Evacuations began on 12 December from Anzac and Suvla and were completed by the 19 December without a single loss of life. The troops at Cape Helles started to be moved in January 1916. Most had been evacuated by 7 January, but there were still 19,000 remaining and, that afternoon, the Germans, having been surprised by the previous evacuations, realised what was happening and mounted an artillery bombardment. It went on for some four hours and the Turks were instructed to attack. Astonishingly, they refused to do so. They saw no necessity if the Allies were leaving anyway. By 9 January, the troops were all away. This time there was just one casualty, a naval rating was hit as his ship left shore by a piece of debris from an explosion caused by one of the Allies' time-fused bombs used to blow up munitions dumps.

The Royal Navy maintained a base at Murdos and it was from there that two RNAS aircraft bombed Constantinople in April 1916. Little damage was caused but they had more success bombing in the summer of 1916 when the Turkish destroyer *Yadighiar-i-Milet* sustained serious damage. They also attacked their old renamed adversaries *Selim* and *Midilli* from the air.

The only redeeming features of the whole campaign were the evacuation and the courage of the troops, especially the ANZACs. There were also some lessons and experience gained that would prove useful to the navy in terms of submarine action and in the use of the Royal Naval Air Service.

After the Dardanelles, British and French forces were reduced in the Eastern Mediterranean as submarine warfare increased. However, there were still some small campaigns such as the French patrol of the coast of Syria and Lebanon with a base on the island of Raud off the Lebanon coast. They also occupied the island of Castelorizo off the Turkish coast and other islands were used to gather intelligence.

The British also wished to maintain some kind of presence in Turkey and de Robeck, with his much reduced squadron, was responsible for instigating cattle raids on the coast of Anatolia. Stealing livestock was rather an unusual job for the Royal Navy but the beasts were believed to be for food supply to Germany. De Robeck used Greek irregulars to assist him, as there were no available British troops. The raids began in March 1916 and went on until the following October. The cattle were successfully rustled but ultimately there was little impact on Turkey and the Greek government, concerned about reprisal attacks on Greeks living on the mainland while their troops were involved, objected. There were to be no more major naval campaigns in the Mediterranean.

Mesopotamia 1914–1918

Turkey's entry into the war on the side of Germany had far-reaching implications for the Allies in other places than the Dardanelles. Ultimately, it also led to campaigns in Egypt and Palestine, Macedonia and Mesopotamia (present day Iraq). Mesopotamia, part of the Ottoman Empire, was crucial to the Allied effort as a major supplier of oil to Britain, mostly through the Anglo-Persian Oil Company at Abadan Island in the Shatt-al-Arab. In 1914, when relations with Turkey were deteriorating and the Germans were spreading anti-British propaganda in Mesopotamia, the British government moved quickly and secretly set up a force in the Persian Gulf. However, it was made up of old vessels that might have been capable of dealing with any Turkish vessels in the vicinity but would have been easily overcome by the German cruisers *Emden* and *Königsberg* when they were at large in the Indian Ocean. Therefore *Ocean*, another older vessel but a battleship, commanded by Captain Hayes-Sadler, was also sent out to the Gulf. Indian troops were sent to Bahrain, where the Sheik was sympathetic to British operations, and initially the Indian Government, with Royal Navy support, was responsible for operations in the Gulf. The troops, under the command of Brigadier Delamain, reached Bahrain on 23 October 1914 but, when the Turkish navy attacked the Russians in the Black Sea, they were ordered to the Shatt-al-Arab, and another brigade, Force D, was sent to the Gulf. The Indian troops silenced the guns at the Fao at the entrance to Shatt-al-Arab, where a small garrison was left, while Delamain's 10th Brigade set up camp about two and a half miles away from the Anglo-Persian Oil Company's refinery. The Navy light-armed sloop *Espiegle* was stationed to protect the refinery.

The main objective was to protect the oil pipeline and capturing the port of Basra was seen as essential, since it was the main outlet for the area. It was essentially an Army campaign but the Navy had an important role in that the action was along the rivers Euphrates and Tigris. The main aim was achieved when reinforcements under Lieutenant General Sir AA Bartlett arrived to join Delamain's troops. They advanced on 19 November and, by 22 November, the troops, along with the Royal Navy ships *Espiegle, Odin* and the paddle steamer *Lawrence*, had taken the port. The British agent in Basra, Sir Percy Cox, was keen that they should capitalise on the victory and push on further to Baghdad but the Government of India, considering the limited number of troops and the difficulties in communications, felt that it was too soon. A compromise was reached whereby it was agreed that the troops would advance as far as Kurnah which, being a point where the rivers Euphrates and Tigris joined, was a strategically sound location to guard the whole of the Shatt-al-Arab. Again the *Espiegle* and *Odin* were alongside, although the *Odin* damaged her rudder in the shallow waters and much of the support work was undertaken by paddle steamers and river gunboats. On 9 December Kurnah was taken and the Turkish commandant captured.

In March 1915, the Navy was also involved in attempting to cut off Turkish supplies carried down the Euphrates. A flotilla was put together including two armed river steamers, a barge with a 4-inch gun, tugs and motorboats and, in the main, they were successful in pursuing dhows that carried the supplies through the uncharted river. However, the Turks were building up their troops in Mesopotamia and the British realised that they would need to strengthen their own position. Another Indian brigade was diverted to the area and the sloop *Clio* was sent in a bid to maintain control of the area. The priority was still to protect the oilfields and pipelines but the British also wanted to capture Baghdad. The British and Indian troops succeeded in counteracting the threat to Basra from the reinforced Turkish force.

Following on from this success, the aim was to take Amara where there was a possibility of intercepting retreating Turkish troops. By collecting numerous *bellums* – native wooden canoes – the operation was turned into an amphibious one. It was an unusual campaign for the Royal Navy as the flotilla took the place of cavalry. Along with the *bellums* were the three sloops as well as two launches fitted with sweeps, two gun barges, two armed horse boats and a large flotilla of smaller vessels. Starting on 31 May, the troops achieved great success, securing Amara within four days. There was growing confidence and, indeed, operations in Mesopotamia had been some of the most successful of the war. This led to the decision to push for a capture of Baghdad which, if achieved, would effectively cut German communications with Persia and Afghanistan.

There was a delay in waiting for permission to go ahead from London and also because the river was at low water. The Navy sent out HMS *Firefly*, the first of the new Fly-class vessel which were gunboats ordered by Fisher that had been originally intended for working in the Danube. However, the flotilla was unable to be of much assistance to the soldiers as they tried to break through the Turkish troops in November because the banks were too high and the gunboats were vulnerable to artillery attack. The army under Townshend was forced to retreat and the flotilla, in assisting the troops, lost a launch that ran aground. Then, on 1 December, *Firefly* was significantly damaged by artillery fire. The tug that tried to save her ran aground and both had to be abandoned. By 9 December, Townshend and his army were besieged at the town of Kut. Between January and April of the following year, there were continual but unsuccessful attempts to relieve them. More Fly-class vessels were deployed along with *Mantis*, a large gunboat, but really much more powerful resources were required if they were to have any effect. The river steamer *Julnar* made a desperate effort to get supplies into Kut but she came under Turkish fire and ran aground. Her commander was killed by a shell and her second-in-command was murdered by the Turks after capture. It had been hoped that success at Baghdad would recover some of the prestige lost in the Dardanelles but, on 29 April 1916, Townshend was forced to surrender.

In February 1916, during the siege, the War Office took

over control of the Mesopotamian campaign from the Government of India. In August 1916, Lieutenant General Sir Stanley Maude was made commander-in-chief of the Mesopotamian Expeditionary Force with instructions to maintain British control of Basra and the surrounding area and, in February 1917, he finally re-took Kut. It was decided to renew efforts to take Baghdad. In the meantime, the flotilla had been guarding lines of communication against raids and had been reinforced with the additional gunboats, *Tarantula* and *Moth*. They took part in the advance, again acting as cavalry, and suffered heavy fire and many casualties but they battled through. In their retreat the Turks left behind the previously abandoned *Firefly* and she was taken back into the flotilla along with a Turkish steamer and a tug. The gunboats caused great panic amongst the Turkish army, sending many into flight. At last, on 11 March, Baghdad was occupied by the British and they took control of the Mosul oilfields.

Submarines and The Baltic

The Creation of the British Submarine Service

In 1904, when Fisher was first appointed First Lord of the Admiralty, he was perceptive in realising the potentially important role that the submarine would have in future warfare. Although his predecessor, Selbourne, had ordered the building of submarines, their role was unclear and there was much opposition to the service being set up at all. There were those in the Navy who felt that submarines were somehow un-British and that they were the weapons of weaker nations. However, in 1901, *Holland 1* was launched, although the acquisition came after most of the other world navies already had submarines and the design itself was an American one. Vickers Maxim in Barrow-in-Furness built the *Hollands* under licence from American Holland. Within the navy itself, the submariners all volunteered for the service and were somewhat separate from the main service with a reputation as 'unwashed chauffeurs'. The First World War would completely change this attitude.

The first submarines, as we have seen, were the same as

the American vessels since the Admiralty had made no investment in submarine design. However, this rapidly changed and early experimentation led to the development of the D-class submarine in 1907. This had a surface speed of 15 knots, about double the capacity of the Holland, and was 500 tons. This led to the development of the E-class submarine which also had torpedo tubes, was capable of long distance work and was more than a match for contemporary U-boats. In 1910, Roger Keyes was appointed as inspecting captain of submarines and displayed both great enthusiasm for the service and the ability to inspire others. He travelled abroad to look at innovations in submarine and periscope design in order to improve British design. At the beginning of the war, the British had 74 submarines, which outnumbered the Germans, but the German submarines were more up-to-date. Many of the British submarines were old vessels used for coastal operations. The capacity for long range work had certainly not been appreciated when war broke out and both sides envisaged the submarine as a defensive rather than an offensive instrument of war. At the outbreak of war, the most modern of the British submarines were based with Keyes at Harwich in the 8th Flotilla. He also had five other flotillas made up of older vessels. There were in addition three submarines apiece in Malta, Gibraltar and China.

Keyes led several operations at the beginning of the war around Heligoland Bight, taking the submarines and gathering intelligence. However, he also needed destroyers to accompany them because of the submarines' lack of vision.

Lieutenant-Commander Max Horton, who would also become important during the Second World War, made the first significant hit for the British from a submarine on 12 September 1914 when he torpedoed the German cruiser *Hela*. British submarines were also effective in the Sea of Marmara during the Dardanelles campaign. In the opening months of the war, it was not only the Germans that proved the threat and destruction that a small number of submarines could cause.

The Baltic

Horton also played an important role in the Baltic campaign. In so far as the Baltic is a closed sea that could easily be blocked by mines, the geography made it particularly dangerous to surface vessels but submarines could penetrate it. The passages to the sea were in the neutral waters of Denmark and Sweden but the Germans had a major advantage in the Kaiser Wilhelm Canal (the Kiel Canal), which meant they could pass into the sea unimpeded. In contrast, the British and French, in order to reach Russia, their ally, had to make their way via Norway and the north Russian ports. The main concern of the Russians was to protect St Petersburg and hence their naval force was concentrated in the Gulf of Finland. Fisher had envisaged a Baltic campaign at the beginning of the war, essentially with the aim of supporting a Russian invasion of Germany. The Germans did not envisage the Baltic as a main arena and deployed many of their older vessels there, but their crucial interest in the area was to maintain their supply of iron ore from Swedish ports. Not only was this an attractive target for the Allies but also the High Seas Fleet used the Baltic for exercises and so, if it was possible to penetrate, there was the possibility of destroying German naval vessels.

Consequently, Keyes made a proposal to Jellicoe in October 1914 that he should send some of his submarines into the Baltic, which was accepted. Keyes selected three of his most gifted submarine commanders for the opera- tion – Max Horton in *E9*, Noel Laurence in *E1* and Martin Nasmith in *E11*. The plan was for them to penetrate the Baltic at night so that there would be less chance of the German patrol spotting them between Rugen and the Swedish coast. They were to search for the High Seas Fleet and attack it, before making for the Russian port of Libau. Both *E1* and *E9* entered the sea safely, although they were obliged to make anchorage in the Gulf of Finland. The Russians, who had expected a German attack on the port, had virtually destroyed facilities at Libau themselves. *E11*, having been spotted and harassed by German destroyers, decided to return to base. The two submarines that had made it through were placed under the command of the Russian commander-in-chief, Admiral Essen, and they worked with the Russian submarines and in minelaying operations. There were some technical problems with the British submarines and it was difficult for spare parts to be transported to them, a state of affairs not helped by the harsh winter conditions in the Baltic. Both submarines survived but there was no real success in 1914. The presence of the submarines did lead the Germans to withdraw some of large warships that had been giving gunnery support to the army but little more. However, in the spring of 1915, the submarines really began to make their mark.

The Russians and the British submarines were up against two German forces comprising both cruisers and destroyers. One of them made an attack on Libau, not knowing that the port had been evacuated, and a mine sank the German flagship. Horton had some success with an escorted transport convoy, managing to sink one of the transports, and he also intercepted two German battleships and disabled one of them with a torpedo. However, the Russians were still under considerable pressure and reinforcements were dispatched to the Baltic from Harwich. One of those sent out, *E13*, unfortunately had problems with her compass and ran aground on Danish sandbanks. Under international law she had to move and could be offered no assistance, and a group of German destroyers took unfair advantage of the submarine. They torpedoed her and opened machine gun fire at the crew even as they were trying to leap to safety from the submarine. They stopped firing only when a Danish vessel sailed between them. Meanwhile Laurence was having more luck. The German battle-cruiser squadron passed him and he torpedoed and damaged the *Moltke*. The hit led to the Germans withdrawing from an attack on their target, Riga.

On 5 October *E8* made her first hit, destroying a

steamer after her crew had been taken off. On 22 October, she also took the cruiser *Prinz Adalbert*. On 11 October, *E19* had also been successful in sinking four ore-carriers and in forcing another to run aground which subsequently sank. On 18 and 19 October, Horton sank another four merchant vessels. The force might have been even more effective at preventing ore reaching Germany if the Russians had agreed to convene prize courts for neutral ships that were stopped under suspicion of having German-owned cargo. All attacks by the British submarines adhered to the international law regarding the taking of prizes and they gave warning before sinking, giving crews time to reach safety.

The Russians were disappointed when, in December 1915, Horton and Laurence were recalled. They were particularly sad to see Horton go, even making a proposal to the Admiralty that he stay as the Senior Naval Officer of the Baltic. It was not to be. But the other submarines stayed and went out again in the spring of 1916 when the Germans had implemented a convoy system with a large number of torpedo boats. There were still some minor successes but the end of the campaign owed as much to the Russians as the Germans. Discontent had spread through the Baltic fleet as momentum grew towards the 1917 revolution. In addition, the Germans had developed the depth charge, although all the British submarines managed to escape it. The submarine flotilla, under Commander Cromie, now numbered seven but it looked as if they were going to be forced to surrender after the Russian

Revolution. Cromie decided to send the crews back to Britain and scuttled the submarines. He himself stayed at the British Embassy in St Petersburg as the Naval Attaché where he was killed during the Revolution by a group of Bolsheviks as he attempted to defend the building single-handed.

Submarine action in the Dardanelles campaign, discussed in the previous chapter, also enjoyed some success. Between May 1915 and January 1916 the tally for submarines there was two battleships, a destroyer, two gunboats and seven transports in addition to 197 assorted smaller vessels. As in the Baltic, losses were minimal.

The other way in which submarines were employed was as fleet submarines. The British believed that using submarines was the best method of countering enemy submarines. They were therefore used as a screen for the fleet, although initially there was a major problem with this policy in that the submarines were too slow, even when travelling on the surface, to keep pace with the fleet. This led to the development of the steam-propelled K-class submarine, with the first one commissioned in 1916 and another 17 following by the end of the war. On the surface they could make a speed of 25 knots which was sufficient to keep up with the fleet, although there were some disadvantages in that they were slow in diving and their three collapsible smoke stacks were easy to recognise. Trials showed up more problems. The heat in the engine rooms was almost unbearable and *K13* was lost when the boiler room ventilators were not closed properly and flooded.

She continued to go down after the order to blow the tanks. There were 49 survivors out of the 80 on board. She was refloated sometime later. Further trials brought little success. In a fleet exercise in the Firth of Forth they went down like dominoes. K4 was accidentally rammed by K6, then K17 was rammed by *Fearless* which sank her and was then itself rammed by *Inflexible*. An improved K-class was designed but not ordered until after the war and, in the event, only one was subsequently built.

Over the course of the war, the British came to appreciate the value of submarine warfare and did use it effectively in limited arenas. In fact, they used many of the same tactics as the Germans and, at the beginning of the war, they had a larger number of submarines than the German Navy, despite having been slow to embrace them at the beginning of the century. However, it was the Germans who would use submarines most extensively and to most devastating effect. In the British merchant marine they had the perfect target.

Between the Battle of Dogger Bank and the Battle of Jutland (dealt with in the following chapter) there were no meetings between the Grand Fleet and the High Seas Fleet. The major engagement of the two fleets that had been anticipated since the beginning of the war did not appear to be on the horizon and it was a frustrating 18 months. After the Battle of Dogger Bank, when Admiral Pohl replaced Ingenohl as the commander of the High Seas Fleet, the German policy of caution in risking their fleet continued. The British maintained their distant blockade, effectively limiting essential supplies to Germany. Importantly, as Paul Halpern emphasises in his *A Naval History of World War One,* 'The British *did not have to fight* or risk the Grand Fleet to maintain that blockade. The Germans would have to come to them if they wanted to break it.' There were two main reasons why so far the German fleet had not come out – the Kaiser's wish to protect his Navy and the German intention of reducing the numbers of British ships so that Germany would have the numerical advantage should the two fleets engage. In 1915, the Germans had still not achieved their aim, at least not enough to be certain of victory, and they were looking for a new strategy.

A German admiralty staff officer, Korvettenkapitain Wolfgang Wegener, advocated concentration in the Baltic where they already had control, occupation of Denmark where they could coal, and eventually the establishment of bases in the Faeroes, Norway, France and the Azores. The ideas gained some mileage as they were widely distributed around the fleet in memoranda but Tirpitz was largely against them, especially since Wegener did not see submarine warfare as central to gaining maritime supremacy. Tirpitz himself, however, was not clear about the way forward. He advocated an attack on British commerce to include submarine blockade, mining, aircraft attacks on London as well as cruiser warfare in the Atlantic. Tirpitz was inconsistent, changing his mind about cruiser warfare and deciding it would not be so effective, and at the same time he attacked other senior commanders. For both these reasons, he became increasingly ostracised from his peers and lost the confidence of the Kaiser.

German submarine activity was increased in response to what they perceived as British and French violations of international law, for example the laying of mines at the entrance to the Channel and the seizing of German trade vessels carrying food supplies. The British and French maintained the moral advantage inasmuch as their capture of vessels did not generally involve loss of life which submarine attacks on British commerce did. On 4 February 1915, Germany made a declaration that all the waters around Britain and Ireland were now a war zone where any merchant ship would be destroyed without necessarily ensuring the safety of any passengers or crew. They also refused to guarantee the safety of neutral shipping within the area, which led to diplomatic condemnation, not least from the United States. The campaign had to be toned down so that neutral shipping, as long as it was recognised as such, would be immune. The naval leaders felt that the campaign was ruined because the compromises included the sparing of neutrals, hospital ships unless they were carrying troops, and ships of the Belgian Relief fund. These would limit the effectiveness of preventing foreign supplies reaching Britain. Nevertheless it is considered the first unrestricted submarine campaign and it began on 28 February with just 37 submarines, not all of them operational. Some, including Tirpitz, felt that the decision was premature since the number of submarines available was only around a third of the total and, while further ones had been commissioned, new building was slow. Submarine commanders however were instructed to proceed with the utmost energy.

Between March and May 1915, German submarines were responsible for sinking 115 ships, equalling 255,000 gross tons of merchant shipping. Their losses were minimal and, although the British Auxiliary Patrols were out valiantly every day, they were largely powerless because of the size of the area that they were attempting to protect. British mines also proved ineffective due to a design defect. As a result, the British began to arm merchantmen and ordered them to run at hostile submarines to force them into diving.

Although the German submarines were effective, the results of the campaign had an adverse effect on the country's propaganda around the world. Early in the campaign a Norwegian oil tanker travelling from the United States to the Netherlands was hit by a torpedo without the submarine giving warning. It was not sunk and was towed into port. The Germans later had to pay compensation. A Swedish coal steamer was not so lucky; while trading between the Tyne and Las Palmas, she was torpedoed, again without warning, with the loss of nine of her crew. As time went on there were further Dutch, Greek and American casualties. All of these caused diplomatic friction for Germany but the most significant and best known of these incidents was the sinking of the Cunard liner *Lusitania*. On 7 May 1915, Kapitanleutnant Walter Schweiger torpedoed her in the western approaches off the coast of Ireland, just as she was nearing home from New York. It took just one torpedo, although there were reports of two explosions, and she sank with the loss of 1,201 lives. Schweiger may well have thought that she was carrying troops. Although this was not the case, she was certainly carrying ammunition and there has been much discussion since on the nature and quantity of the arms that she had on board. There have also been claims that Churchill orchestrated the sinking to encourage American entry into the war on the Allied side. The argument is that the liner was moving at a slow pace that put her at a greater risk than necessary – especially surprising since *Lusitania* and her sister vessel the *Mauretania* (which held the Blue Ribbon for the fastest Atlantic crossing) were renowned for their speed. However, the shock of the sinking went round the world and its reception was comparable to the news of the loss of the *Titanic*. The Germans were vilified because not only were the casualties civilians but also many of them were women and children. It was only one factor behind the later entry of the USA into the war but it certainly swayed American public opinion in favour of the Allied cause, especially since 128 of those that died were American citizens. While the British policy of blockade lost the Americans money, the German policy of unrestricted submarine warfare lost them innocent lives. The Germans justified the sinking, arguing that the German consulate in New York had published statements to the effect that American citizens travelled on the vessel at their own risk. They also pointed out the fact that, when the submarine captain realised the number of people on board, he desisted from firing a second torpedo. This did nothing to reverse public opinion.

Then, on 19 August, the liner *Arabic* was torpedoed, again off the coast of Ireland, with many casualties, including, on this occasion, three American citizens. This broke the new assurances that Germany had made to America about passenger vessels and President Wilson called for action that would virtually ban submarine activity against merchant shipping. From 30 August onwards, the Germans did agree not to attack any passenger vessels, regardless of the flag that they were flying. Eager to keep open communications with the USA to prevent her entering the war on the side of the Allies, they also proposed a special service for American citizens to make transatlantic crossings in marked vessels, with advance warnings, that would be safe from submarine attack. The Americans refused and the Germans later withdrew submarines from the western waters and turned their attention to minelaying in the North Sea and deploying submarines in the Mediterranean where there was very little in the way of American shipping. In effect, this saw the end of the first submarine campaign against commercial shipping.

The new restriction did little to alter the success of submarine attacks on commercial shipping in general, although British measures against them were beginning to have more effect. They were using nets and sweeps with charges and there were experiments with depth charges.

They implemented the use of Q-ships, which were decoys, often tramp vessels and occasionally sailing vessels that appeared defenceless and easy targets. However, they were armed and could destroy a submarine at close range. Not only were guns installed on trawlers but some of these ships also worked in tandem with British submarines. The trawler would tow the submarine and stay in contact via a telephone link. If the trawler sighted an enemy, it would inform the submarine which would attempt to destroy the U-boat. However, losses were still high and had it not been for the State Insurance Scheme it is possible that the Germans would have succeeded in paralysing British trade. The total loss in tonnage from the German offensive between August 1914 and September 1915 was 1,294,000, although this was very much offset by the building of new vessels and the capture of enemy ships. However, numbers of newly built ships were decreasing and more of them were required for overseas campaigns, so the break in unrestricted submarine warfare gave the Admiralty a little breathing space.

The Germans instigated a second U-boat campaign against commercial shipping on 11 February 1916. There were some restrictions – only merchantmen within the war zone could be sunk without warning, they could only be sunk outside the zone if they were armed vessels and passenger liners were out of bounds. Some in the German naval command felt that the campaign could never be effective while there were these restrictions in place. U-boat commanders would either be over cautious and consequently let their prey escape, or their enthusiasm would lead to the sinking of vessels that were exempt which would, in turn, lead to diplomatic conflict. Admiral Henning von Holzendorff, head of the Admiralstab in this new offensive, was supported by his equivalent in the German Army, General Erich von Falkenhayn. Falkenhayn was about to try to weaken the British and French Army with a massive push at Verdun. He did not think that the land campaign alone would prove decisive in forcing Britain out of the war, but he hoped that, in conjunction with an increased pressure at sea, it might be brought about. Also in February 1916, von Pohl died from cancer and was replaced as the commander of the High Seas Fleet by the more aggressive Vice Admiral Scheer. The Germans came back in greater forces than before, with 52 submarines in comparison to the 29 that were operational at the beginning of the first campaign. Again it would be diplomatic relations that brought the campaign to a halt rather than military intervention.

The Dutch, who were neutral, lost a considerable number of vessels to German torpedoes but it was American relations that Germany was keen to maintain. On 24 March 1916, a torpedo was fired at the French passenger steamer, *Sussex*, on her way to Folkestone. She did not actually sink but there were a number of casualties and this time the Americans issued an ultimatum. Unless this kind of warfare ceased they would close diplomatic communications. Consequently orders went to the German fleet that, providing a ship did not resist, it was not to operate outside the prize law regulations, which included warning a ship before attack and ensuring the safety of those aboard. Scheer was incensed, believing that the campaign could not be successful in the war zone if submarines had to be exposed to danger by declaring themselves in order to warn vessels. He therefore ordered that the submarines withdrew and that the offensive against British merchant shipping was over. Many in the German navy felt Scheer should have been overruled but the Kaiser gave his approval on 30 April 1916. Scheer now had plans to use the submarines in conjunction with the High Seas Fleet and these would ultimately lead to the Battle of Jutland.

The Battle of Jutland

The Battle of Jutland, which involved nearly 250 ships, was easily the largest battle of the First World War and, because there was no submarine action (although submarines had formed part of the original German plan), it has remained the biggest surface-only encounter in the years since.

When Vice Admiral Scheer took over command of the High Seas Fleet, he was determined to pressurize the British into major fleet action in the North Sea and implemented an aggressive programme. Many of the tactics had been used earlier in the war – airship raids, the bombardment of coastal towns, destroyer sweeps, mining and attacks on commercial trade. The Germans intended to use more powerful forces in sweeps and to ensure that the main fleet was available to reinforce them.

On 10 February 1916, a German destroyer flotilla came out with the Tenth Minesweeping Flotilla. A destroyer took a sloop, the *Arabis,* while the minelayers were operating to the east of Dogger Bank. Jellicoe, Beatty and Tyrwhitt went out but not only were they unable to engage with the German destroyers, in addition *Arethusa,* Tyrwhitt's flagship, was struck by a mine and sank on the way back.

Scheer co-ordinated a bigger attack on 5–6 March and brought out the fleet for a sweep as far as Terschelling. Submarines were stationed off the British coast and, at the same time, there were zeppelin attacks on Hull and Immingham. Scheer had hoped that he would be able to catch the Grand Fleet and the Harwich force out on patrols but, when he put out a radio message, it was intercepted and the British patrols were immediately recalled. The British policy remained unchanged, since they did not see that offensive action could possibly be effective unless the High Seas Fleet came out. However, they did take minor offensive actions. Seaplanes from the converted carrier *Vindex*, escorted by the Harwich Force, were used to raid suspected zeppelin sheds at Hoyer. Tyrwhitt was also out and ready to provide reinforcements. Of the five seaplanes only two returned. The others encountered engine problems and had no choice but to land in German territory. As they searched for the aircraft Tyrwhitt's destroyers came under German aircraft fire and encountered two German patrol trawlers which they sank. The Admiralty ordered the British to withdraw on intelligence that the High Seas Fleet was coming out, although, in the event, Scheer only sent out some powerful cruisers and destroyers. A German destroyer was lost to a mine and a second one was rammed and sunk by *Cleopatra*. Unfortunately, *Cleopatra* was then accidentally rammed and badly damaged by *Undaunted*. The Germans picked up news of the incident and they started to move towards the British but, because of bad weather, they were unable to take advantage of the situation.

There was some disagreement between the Admiralty and Jellicoe about whether or not to continue with such raids. The Admiralty felt that there was still a possibility that such activity would draw out the High Seas Fleet. Jellicoe was under pressure to mount another attack but he had reservations. If the Germans did come out under such measures, the battle might take place in an unfavourable location for the British fleet, or it might have to wait for over a day and the destroyers would need refuelling. Nevertheless the British cruisers were sent out for a raid into the Kattegat to interrupt German commercial vessels and to divert their attention from Russians relaying mine-fields. The following day there was news that the High Seas Fleet was preparing to leave port and so the Grand Fleet and the Battle Cruiser Fleet were ordered out. Although, in fact, the Germans were already returning home by this time, there was still a possibility of intercepting their battle cruisers at Horn Reefs. The British went at full speed but they were forced to turn back as heavy fog fell, causing chaos. The collision of two battle cruisers was followed by a collision between three destroyers, and finally a merchant vessel collided with a dreadnought.

On 24–25 April, the German battle cruisers, with the High Seas Fleet ready to back them up, made a raid on Lowestoft, giving the British another potential opportunity to engage them. Again the Grand Fleet and the Battle Cruiser Fleet put to sea and so did Tyrwhitt's force, although its numbers had been reduced because 12 of his destroyers were on a minelaying mission off Flanders.

Tyrwhitt's weakened force came across four German battle cruisers, accompanied by six light cruisers, and he turned south to try to lure the Germans into following him. They declined to take the bait and went on to bombard both Lowestoft and Yarmouth. Nevertheless, Tyrwhitt turned again and engaged them with his inferior force, badly damaging his flagship, *Conquest*, in the process. Despite their advantage, the Germans turned for home. The Grand Fleet had no chance of reaching them in time and the Admiralty became concerned about the raids on the east coast and the incapability of the Grand Fleet or the Battle Cruiser Fleet to intercept German ships as they returned to base. Distance, of course, was a factor with the Grand Fleet in Scapa Flow and the Battle Cruiser Fleet in Rosyth and it was decided that there should be a permanent deployment of ships in the Thames estuary at Swin. It would comprise the Third Battle Squadron, *Dreadnought,* seven *King Edward VII*-class battleships and the Third Cruiser Squadron. In addition, most of the submarines formerly based at Rosyth were moved south to Yarmouth. Although preparations would not be complete until spring 1918, it was also decided in May to move the Grand Fleet from its base further south to the Firth of Forth.

In the meantime, the British continued with raids that were always secondary in their aims to the hope of goading the Germans out to sea. On 4 May the seaplanes *Vindex* and *Engadine* went to raid zeppelin sheds at Tondern and, at the same time, both Jellicoe's and Beatty's forces were at sea. The seaplanes had no better fortune than before. Only three of them actually managed to launch – one crashed when it hit the mast of a destroyer, one had a faulty engine and had to return and a third did manage to bomb Tondern but missed the shed, and was shot down by a zeppelin. The other eight planes failed on take off and had to be lifted from the sea. Jellicoe waited in hope of the German fleet leaving base and, after about six hours, turned back, disappointed again.

Towards the end of May both fleets had plans for another raid. Jellicoe's plan was to send two light cruiser squadrons on 2 June on a sweep around the Skaw to the Kattegat and south to the Great Belt and the Sound. There was also to be considerable support. Both Beatty and Jellicoe would be northwest should the Germans come out north from Heligoland, a battle squadron was to be stationed in the Skaggerak and there would be submarines off Dogger Bank and the south of Horns Reef where the minefields were to be extended. Also at Horns Reef the seaplane carrier *Engadine*, with a light cruiser squadron and destroyers, would look out for zeppelins. Scheer, on the other hand, was planning to bombard Sunderland with cruisers, with the High Seas Fleet to the south of Dogger Bank, and eighteen submarines placed off the British bases. Since the intention was to draw out the British fleet to the cruisers after the submarines had attacked, Scheer planned zeppelin reconnaissance to make sure that the fleet was not already at sea. Poor weather conditions meant that the zeppelins could not go out, but he could not delay too long because the U-boats could only stay for a limited time without needing to refuel or expose themselves. Scheer therefore decided against the bombardment and instead ordered a sweep on British patrols, ordering the cruisers to make themselves conspicuous near the Norwegian coast so that their presence would be reported and encourage a British interception.

At 1am on 31 May, Hipper left port at Jade with his battle cruisers, while Scheer and the best part of the High Seas Fleet sailed just afterwards. The British ships were already at sea, having received intelligence the day before that the Germans were preparing to leave port. Jellicoe and Beatty had been ordered to concentrate in the Long Forties. Jellicoe, in his flagship *The Iron Duke*, had 24 dreadnoughts, 3 battle cruisers, 12 light cruisers, 8 armoured cruisers, 5 flotilla leaders, 46 destroyers and a minelayer. Beatty had 6 battle cruisers, 4 dreadnoughts, 14 light cruisers, 27 destroyers and a seaplane carrier. The Germans under Hipper had 5 battle cruisers, 4 light cruisers and 30 destroyers. Scheer was following with 16 dreadnoughts, 6 pre-dreadnoughts, 5 light cruisers and 31 destroyers. The British had a clear advantage in numbers.

Although intelligence had been invaluable in warning the British Fleet of the imminent sailing of the High Seas Fleet, a mix-up in communications meant that Jellicoe was told at 12.30pm that the Germans were still at the Jade. Assuming that time was on his side, he sailed at a moderate pace so as not to waste fuel and slowed to examine neutral ships. He was therefore taken by surprise when he came across the High Seas Fleet just a few hours later. The mistake had far reaching implications. Had he made his rendezvous with Beatty earlier they would have had the advantage of more daylight. It also meant that Jellicoe would treat further intelligence messages with great circumspection and this affected the decisions that he would make during the battle.

When the two fleets encountered each other it was almost by accident. At around 2pm, two of Beatty's light cruisers, *Galatea* and *Phaeton*, spotted a Danish steamer that had come to a halt and went closer to investigate. They then sighted Hipper's cruiser *Elbing* which was doing the same thing. They reported the German presence and opened fire just before 2.30pm. Although two of Beatty's light cruiser squadrons headed towards the action, Beatty changed course to the south-east some 12 minutes later with the aim of intercepting the Germans and preventing their return to the Bight. Unfortunately, Evan-Thomas of the Fifth Battle Squadron did not see the flag signal to turn, resulting in a ten-mile gap opening up between Beatty and Evan-Thomas. The latter only turned when the signal was repeated using searchlights which should have been used in conjunction with the original signal.

An hour later, *Lion* sighted Hipper's force and Beatty turned east at full speed to prevent them reaching the Bight. Shortly afterwards, a plane was launched from *Engadine* but the weather conditions prevented it from transmitting knowledge of the sighting by searchlight. Technical problems forced the plane to land and the weather prevented further launches. The *Engadine* did not have sufficient speed capacity to keep up with the fleet and so was not able to participate further. Even so, the incident was notable as the first time that a seaplane had taken part in a fleet action. The intention had also been to use the carrier *Campania*, based in Scapa, with Jellicoe but she had not received the signal to leave port. In the end, she left too late. With no possibility of catching up with the fleet and possibly vulnerable to submarine attack, she was ordered back to base.

As soon as Hipper knew that he had been sighted, he turned 180 degrees to try to draw the British to the High Seas Fleet. Both sides opened fire at 3.48pm and both over-estimated the range. The Fifth Battle Squadron was still over 7 miles away and Jellicoe was about 53 miles away. The High Seas Fleet was still 46 miles away from Hipper. So at this point there were six British ships and five German vessels. There were more mistakes as a result of missed signals. Beatty intended that each British ship should take its opposite number and that *Lion* and *Princess Royal*, leading the squadron, should concentrate on Hipper's flagship *Lützow*. However, as some ships did not see the signal or misinterpreted it, the second German ship *Derfflinger* was not engaged for over ten minutes. Historians have debated the significance of this mistake in the final outcome of the battle but it is possible that it was not as important as first thought. Although overall German firing in the initial stages of the battle was faster and more accurate than the British, *Derfflinger's* fire at the beginning was not effective. Weather conditions were partly responsible for giving the Germans an advantage, allowing them better visibility, and the wind direction blew most of the smoke towards the British ships.

Lützow hit *Lion* on her midships Q turret, nearly causing her loss through flash, putting her out of action at 4.00pm. At 4.02 *Indefatigable* was blown up and sunk by the *Von der Tann*, and, immediately afterwards, Evan-Thomas arrived with the Fifth Battle Squadron and got in range to attack the *Von der Tann*. Although this arrival reinforced the British forces and put Hipper under pressure, and the superior range finders of the Fifth Battle Squadron improved gunnery accuracy, it was not enough to prevent the loss of the *Queen Mary* at 4.26. The *Derfflinger* hit her with two or three 12-inch shells and she blew up and sank with the loss of all but 20 of her 1,286 crew. Flotilla attacks were ordered on both sides and there was a burst of furious destroyer action, resulting in the loss of *V.27* and *V.29* for Hipper and the loss of the British destroyers *Nestor* and *Nomad*. *Seydlitz* was hit by a British torpedo but did not sustain serious damage. At 4.38 things were about to change when Commodore Goodenough reported the sighting of Scheer and the High Seas Fleet. Goodenough, in the *Southampton*, turned in order to draw the Germans towards Jellicoe. Once again the British had signalling problems and again it was the Fifth Battle Squadron that missed the signal to turn. This time a three mile gap opened up between Evan-Thomas and Beatty. This made Evan-Thomas very vulnerable to the Third Squadron of the High Seas Fleet and the Germans engaged but the Fifth

Battle Squadron was able to escape. This ended the first phase of the battle, sometimes referred to as 'the run to the south', and now Beatty began to draw Scheer and Hipper towards Jellicoe, beginning the 'run to the north'.

The British began to have more success, despite continual problems with visibility, which also affected the Germans after 5.40. Considerable damage was done to Hipper's battle cruisers *Lützow*, *Derfflinger* and *Seydlitz* and, while they remained afloat, their effectiveness was much reduced. The armour on the German ships, often thicker than that of British equivalents, made them very hard to sink and, in addition, the internal divisions within the ships were better for damage control.

At 4.05pm, the Third Battle Cruiser Squadron (*Invincible, Inflexible, Indomitable* with two light cruisers, and four destroyers), under Rear Admiral Hood moved to reinforce Beatty but they went too far to the east. As a result, Hood's light cruiser *Chester* ran into Rear Admiral Boedicker's Second Scouting Group as they were screening Hipper. *Chester* was badly battered before she managed to fall back to Hood's battle cruisers which engaged and disabled *Wiesbaden*. Hipper was still fighting Beatty's force but, seeing Hood, believed that he was dealing with the British battle fleet and made the decision to fall back on Scheer. He had been about to launch a destroyer attack on Beatty but now directed it somewhat ineffectively on Hood. The destroyers did, however, batter the British destroyer *Shark* which later sank. The major advantage of the arrival of Hood's squadron was that it screened

Jellicoe's approach and also drew the German Third Battle Squadron to the east. It was possible that had this Squadron, under Rear Admiral Behncke, carried on its course it might have been in a position to surprise Jellicoe who was approaching at full speed.

Jellicoe was sailing with his three battle squadrons in a cruising formation, which was unsuitable for engagement because the ships masked each other and it was not possible to employ a great number of the heavy guns. He would need time for them to assume a battle formation but he had received no intelligence from Beatty between 4.45 and 6.00 on the position of the Germans and thought that he had time to spare. In addition, when he did get reports, there were errors in the estimate of the enemy positions, which meant that Beatty was much further west than anticipated and the Germans were about to come upon him. At 6.15 he sighted the *Lion* and positioned himself so that he was able to use most of his heavy guns and the Germans could only use a limited number of theirs. Beatty moved across to head the line in front of the British Fleet in his previously prescribed position, although this meant that Jellicoe had to slow down to allow clearance, and the smoke obscured his vision and got in the way of British firing. The Fifth Battle Squadron did not have sufficient speed to follow and therefore took the back of the line. *Warspite* had a lucky escape when her helm jammed and she was forced to circle twice in front of the German dread-noughts as they advanced but, although she came under heavy fire, she did not sustain serious damage. Briefly she was able to manoeuvre but, when the helm jammed again, she was ordered back to port. At the same time Rear Admiral Robert Arbuthnot took the armoured cruisers *Defence* and *Warrior* to engage with the light cruisers of the German Second Scouting Group. They were ferociously attacked by the advancing German ships and, as a result, *Defence* was lost with all hands. *Warrior* managed to escape as *Warspite* diverted German attention. She was taken under tow by *Engadine* but could not be saved and sank the following day.

At 6.20, Hood was in range to fire on Hipper's battle cruisers to great effect. *Lützow* took a battering that eventually saw her loss. However, this was soon followed by the loss of *Invincible* in another incident that saw a hit to the 'Q' turret, resulting in a flash that went directly to the magazines and blew the entire ship. It was a serious design fault in the British battle cruisers. 1,026 men were lost, including Hood himself.

By 6.40, all of the Grand Fleet had been deployed and were able to fire. Scheer was therefore in trouble and ordered what amounted to an about turn, as the German Third Flotilla Squadron mounted a torpedo attack and covered it with a smokescreen at around 6.45. Only the *Marlborough* was hit and she listed but was still operational. It was not immediately obvious to Jellicoe that the Germans had turned away. Not for the first time, he was let down by communications since those that were in a position to see what the Germans were doing did not report it. Once he realised what was happening, he decided to order the fleet not to follow closely, for which he has been much criticised. Instead he ordered it on a course that would ultimately cut the line of retreat to the German bases. Regardless of whether he might have achieved more had he sent some divisions in direct chase of the Germans, he was following the Grand Fleet Battle Orders.

Just before 7.00pm, a second chance came for the British when Scheer, for reasons that are still unclear, ordered another 180-degree turn, putting himself in direct line of Jellicoe's ships. By 7.15, all the British ships were in a position to fire and the German ships at the van came under particularly heavy attack. For the most part, the Germans were unable to see the British ships and Scheer ordered his battle cruisers to head straight for them, but a minute later ordered them to attack the British van so that they went south. The German destroyer flotillas were ordered to make smoke, attack and then turn. In response, Jellicoe ordered a destroyer attack and, until 7.45, they continued to put immense pressure on the Germans, scoring 37 hits to two. However, just as the British were in a position to inflict more serious damage, Jellicoe, again following Grand Fleet Battle Orders, ordered the fleet to turn away. The main justification for this turn was that torpedoes would not be able to inflict as much damage. If the fleet was turning away, the torpedoes would lose effectiveness, hitting the ships at a slower speed by the time they reached them. In addition, had they turned towards the torpedoes, they might have been vulnerable to further torpedoes from other sections of the German lines. There are still those who believe that the losses that Jellicoe sought to avoid may have been worth the sacrifice if it had meant a decisive victory over the High Seas Fleet.

The main battle fleets were not to meet again but smaller engagements went on through the night. Beatty encountered the First Scouting Group and once more outgunned the Germans but, again controversially, he had no backup from any of the battle squadrons. Jellicoe maintained a position between Scheer and the German bases with the intention that battle should be resumed the next day. He wanted to avoid night action at all costs. Apart from his concern about torpedo attacks, the Germans were better equipped to fight in darkness. Their searchlights were larger, protected with shutters and, in conjunction with their gunnery control systems, they could automatically follow the binoculars of the lookout. The British were less technically prepared for night fighting and, in fact, were not trained for this eventuality. Scheer returned to base by the Horns Reef and the Amrun Channel, which was a route that Jellicoe had not envisaged and therefore had not covered. The night encounters were mostly dominated by the Germans because of their superior night-time fighting techniques. British losses were substantial – *Black Prince* (armoured cruiser), *Tipperary* (flotilla leader), as well as the destroyers *Fortune*, *Turbulent* and *Ardent*. *Sparrowhawk* was also lost but she was accidentally rammed by British ships. There were also German losses – the pre-dreadnought *Pommern* was lost outright to a British torpedo. In addition, they had to abandon towing the *Lutzow*, which was limping from action earlier in the day, and two light cruisers were lost as they were rammed by a German dreadnought. The *Rostock* was hit by a British torpedo and needed towing but had to be scuttled later when she came under threat from the cruiser *Dublin*. The destroyer *V4* sank, possibly as a result of hitting a mine.

Although these night skirmishes revealed that Scheer was taking the route via Horns Reef to return to port, no-one thought to inform Jellicoe. Doubtless, he would have not sought a night battle but it would have had a bearing on his subsequent strategy. The intelligence might have still reached him via Room 40 at the Admiralty. Initially they sent an intercepted message reporting the location of the ship at the rear of the German fleet, an error transmitted by the Germans as it turned out, but this was followed by another message that gave the correct location. Probably because of his experience earlier in the day, Jellicoe ignored it. The Admiralty received further intelligence that corroborated the second message but failed to pass this on at all. Had Jellicoe received it, it is more likely that he would have positioned the fleet to resume battle the following day. In the event, he returned to port.

The Germans claimed Jutland as a victory, which was certainly true in terms of losses inflicted. The British lost the three battle cruisers *Queen Mary, Indefatigable* and *Invincible*, the armoured cruisers *Defence, Warrior* and *Black Prince*, the flotilla leader *Tipperary*, the destroyers *Ardent, Nestor, Turbulent, Shark, Nomad* and *Sparrowhawk,* and had a total of 6,094 men killed. The Germans lost the battle cruiser *Lutzow*, the pre-dreadnought *Pommern*, the light cruisers *Wiesbaden, Frauenlob, Elbing* and *Rostock,* the destroyers *V.27, V.29, V.48, S.35* and *V.4*, and had a total of 2,551 men killed. Despite the fact that there were fewer German losses, their Fleet was largely unfit to go to sea. Armour plating had prevented the sinking of many ships but they had sustained considerable damage. However, in terms of strategy, there was no advantage for the Germans who were defeated in the sense that the battle resulted in no change for them. The Grand Sea Fleet was still numerically superior, the Germans were still more or less trapped in port and they had not managed to break the British blockade. Also, even had the Germans suffered heavier losses, it would have made no difference to their submarine capacity to inflict losses upon British commerce. For the British it was obviously disappointing and there was an extensive investigation into the battle, which highlighted many technological deficiencies, particularly in the area of gunnery and ammunition. There was not, for example, adequate protection for preventing flash reaching magazines, British cordite charges were also unsafe and British shells were inefficient. The thickness of armour plating was another factor, which had made British ships more vulnerable than their German counterparts. The generally greater weight of British shell, however, was an advantage as well as the generally superior speed capacity of British battle cruisers.

Scheer believed that, even had they inflicted more severe losses upon the British Fleet, it was unlikely that such an outcome would have induced it to surrender. Therefore, he advocated a return to unrestricted submarine warfare to grind Britain down by attacking trade.

Defeating the U-Boat
and the Final Stages of War

Unrestricted Submarine Warfare

Morale was low after the Battle of Jutland and there was no good news from the Western Front. A few weeks after Jellicoe declared that the Grand Sea Fleet was fit for sea again, the Battle of the Somme would begin on 1 July 1916. On 5 June, there was another blow for British morale when Lord Kitchener was lost at sea on the cruiser *Hampshire* when she hit a German mine off the Orkneys.

It took the High Seas Fleet until August to be seaworthy and on 19 August they came out to raid Sunderland, just as they had intended before the Battle of Jutland. Room 40 performed well on this occasion, informing Jellicoe of German movements so that both he and Beatty were at sea in advance of Scheer. Tyrwhitt's Harwich force was also ordered out to a position off Yarmouth. However, there was to be no fleet action that day. A British patrol submarine torpedoed the *Westfalen,* a German battleship, which was not sunk but sustained enough damage to force her back to port. The wireless signal that she sent confirmed that the Germans were at sea as well as giving away their position.

The information was relayed to Jellicoe, but he did not receive it until later because he had been delayed when *Nottingham* was torpedoed and sunk by *U.52*. When *Nottingham* went down, it was not immediately possible to determine whether it was the result of a mine or a torpedo. Jellicoe wanted to be sure that his ships were not about to enter a minefield so he changed course. The result was a four-hour delay but he may still have been in time to intercept the High Seas Fleet had it not been for a mistake on the part of German intelligence. A zeppelin that had been monitoring the Harwich force reported that it was a strong enemy force with dreadnoughts, although in fact they were light cruisers. Scheer, believing that it was therefore a part of the Grand Fleet, abandoned course for Sunderland and went south. After the sinking of the *Westfalen*, Tyrwhitt had taken a northern course but, failing to find any German ships, then reversed course for base and, in the process, unwittingly turned away from Scheer. Scheer, having heard that the Grand Fleet was, in fact, pursuing him from the north and he was thus too late for a bombardment of Sunderland, also began to head back home. Once Jellicoe knew of the German retreat, he realised that no encounter was possible and he too headed for base, although the British still had to contend with enemy submarines. One of Beatty's light cruisers, *Falmouth*, was torpedoed and sunk the following day while being towed. Tyrwhitt had turned again and had sighted the Germans but, by this time, it was early evening and there was not enough time before darkness fell for him to position himself favourably for an attack.

As a result of the loss of the two battle cruisers that had been part of a screen for the fleet, which could not be reinforced without newly built ships, the British strategy returned to one of great caution in coming out to the south. The distant blockade was still very effective and it began to look more likely that victory could be won without a major fleet battle. Scheer had been keen to try a similar manoeuvre again with a different submarine formation but, for the time being, unfavourable weather conditions prevented him from going ahead with such a plan. By the time that he could have implemented it, the U-boats were re-deployed to attack British trade once again. They were to follow prize rules with the proviso that armed merchantmen could be sunk without warning, even though Scheer believed that only unrestricted submarine warfare would be truly effective. The High Seas Fleet was not to undertake an offensive operation in the North Sea until the spring of 1918.

Scheer, without his submarines, came up with another plan to use his destroyers, with the backup of the High Seas Fleet, to attack merchantmen in the North Sea. The plan came to nothing because British intelligence picked up on his movements and recalled or diverted merchant craft and light forces. Unfavourable weather also prevented the destroyers from going out as far as they had intended, and a British submarine torpedoed *München* which had to be towed back to base. This time the Grand Fleet was on alert but, in accordance with the new policy, it did not leave base. Offensive patrolling was left to the submarines. The

Germans were unable to leave port without being detected by British submarines but Scheer, deprived of the use of his own submarines, was unable to glean the same information about the British Fleet coming out.

By November 1916, the resumption of submarine attacks on British commerce was resulting in the loss of over 120,000 tons per month, more than double the monthly averages that the Germans had achieved in the campaigns earlier in the year. The Germans had introduced larger and more powerful submarines in the UB.II boats that made up the Flanders Flotilla in the latter part of 1916. They were a large contributory factor to the increased rate in sinkings. Another factor in the German success was the greater availability of submarines in comparison to the number operational at the beginning of 1916. The range of their activity was also greatly increased, including operations as far as the coast of North America and a successful raid into the Arctic. The Germans also broke their earlier promise of not attacking passenger liners when the P&O liner *Arabia* was torpedoed in the Mediterranean on 6 November 1916, although all the passengers were saved when other ships rushed to her aid. The only casualties were engine room staff. This incident, together with some other lost ships, again involved American citizens but what was of even greater concern to the USA were submarine operations within American waters.

At home in Britain, the Navy was coming under criticism for this as well as the inconclusive Battle of Jutland

and the First Lord of the Admiralty, Jackson, was replaced by Jellicoe. For the fleet, the highly popular Jellicoe was a sad loss and he showed some reluctance to leave for London himself. Although there were several potential candidates for the post who were senior to him, Beatty was made Commander-in-Chief of the Grand Fleet. Having performed well at Jutland, he was a popular public choice.

The new board in London would be occupied primarily with the submarine threat. The long game of the blockade was increasing pressure on the German home front and their failure to make headway on the Western Front was leading to a financial breakdown. The Germans were desperately looking for a solution and were determined once more to break British trade. This time it would be the unrestricted submarine warfare that Scheer had long been advocating. The Germans now felt that the concessions that they had made in trying to keep their diplomatic channels open with America were preventing them from achieving victory. Despite the heavy losses of British merchant vessels, overall numbers still equated to 94 per cent of the total at the start of the war. In a memorandum of December 1916, Holtzendorf, chief of the Admiralstab, set out his argument for unrestricted submarine warfare and the campaign began on 1 February 1917.

The German high command prioritised submarine construction and, throughout 1917, they never had less than 105 operational submarines. At some points, they had as many as 129. There were plans for further construction to be ready in 1918 and 1919 as hopes for a swift conclusion to the war began to look less realistic.

The submarine blockade of Britain extended roughly from the Dutch coast to the Norwegian coast, nearly as far as the Faeroe Islands and to Cape Finisterre. In addition, the submarines also covered routes into the Arctic Ocean. These waters in what the Germans referred to as *Sperrgebeit* were declared closed to shipping and neutrals using them were told that they did so at their own risk. There were some minor concessions – one American steamer each week would be allowed into Falmouth, and one Dutch steamer per day could operate between Flushing and Harwich, as long as they were appropriately marked with red and white stripes and a red and white checked flag. The entire Mediterranean was also declared a prohibited zone, although initially a small corridor was designated free to enable neutral Spain and Greece (neutral at this point) to continue trading. Ships from these two nations were not immune but prize rules were followed in the area until November 1917 when the concession was cancelled. It was not long before the German campaign alienated the Americans altogether. They demonstrated their disapproval almost immediately by cutting off diplomatic channels on 3 February. By April, following the sinking of more passenger liners, notably the *Laconia* and the *Algonquin*, and the revelation by British intelligence that the Germans were endeavouring to make alliances with Mexico and Japan, America was finally forced into the war. War was declared on Germany on 6 April, although the declaration did not include Austria-Hungary. With immediate effect, any German vessels were retained in American ports. The Germans hoped that American intervention would arrive too late to have any impact on the outcome of the war.

Even though the campaign was not breaking British commerce as quickly as the Germans had envisaged, the losses were savage. In the early months of 1917, they increased from 520,412 tons in February to 860,334 tons in April. Although the April figure was never to be matched again, had such a rate of losses continued Britain would have been crippled by November 1917.

The Germans also succeeded in bringing neutral shipping to a virtual standstill as ship owners kept their ships in neutral ports and refused to let them sail. In order to ensure that she could still receive essential imports, Britain imposed harsh counter-measures. She refused to let neutral vessels sail from British ports unless they agreed that they would not head for a neutral port where they would be laid up. If they were trading with a neutral port, they were only allowed to leave the UK if they agreed to return with an approved cargo to a British or another Allied port. In the case of Dutch or Scandinavian vessels, they were only permitted to leave British ports on the arrival of an equivalent vessel with the same flag. However, no matter how Britain forced neutrals to continue to supply her ports, it was of little use if the ships were sunk by submarines, and they had to look for other solutions. There were some precautions already in place. Ships carrying essential supplies, for example, were directed to sail on predetermined routes patrolled with destroyers, sloops and trawlers. Merchantmen also travelled overnight, were kept as close to the shoreline as possible, were backed up with patrols and were dispersed from their usual routes and ports. They were directed by naval officers and, as far as possible, intelligence was used so that traffic could be diverted when the authorities were aware of submarine threats. Earlier in the war, these kinds of measures had been reasonably effective but now, with far more intensive warfare and terrifying losses, they were completely inadequate. The question of how to protect merchant shipping dominated Admiralty discussions, aided by the newly formed Anti-Submarine Division set up by Jellicoe in December 1916. The instinct at the Admiralty was for offensive action using hunting patrols and Q-ships, as favoured by Jellicoe, together with nets, mines and depth charges. There were also experiments with new technology such as hydrophones. At the beginning of the war, the British had held back on laying minefields because they might restrict trade and the first minefield was not laid until early 1915. Beatty now called for intensive minelaying, especially around the Bight. There was a difficulty with a shortage of mines and the design fault that had made British mines unreliable since the beginning of the war was still a problem. Beatty scaled down his plan and, although a copy of the German mine had been ordered in 1916, this would not be ready until late 1917. During the second half of 1917, the mines proved quite successful, destroying 11 U-boats, but these results were still not enough to really counteract the German threat.

The other option was considered defensive. This was a return to the traditional convoy system that was already being used to protect troop ships. There was opposition to convoy because the concentration of vessels in one area made them potentially even more vulnerable to submarine attack. It would also tie up large numbers of them and slow many of them down as they would all have to travel at the speed of the slowest ship. However, as huge losses continued and other measures showed disappointing results, the Admiralty came under increasing pressure to implement a convoy system. To Beatty's immense frustration, Jellicoe was vehemently against convoy. Jellicoe's doggedness on this point would lead to him losing office at the end of 1917. At the end of April, convoys were introduced, initially on a relatively small scale to cover Dutch routes around the Hook of Holland, the French coal trade and Scandinavian trade. They proved very successful and the policy was expanded. America's entry into the war helped the situation since the Americans provided additional vessels, firstly for patrols and subsequently on convoy duties. By the end of August 35 American destroyers were based in Queenstown, Ireland, and played a vital role in the success of the convoy system. Earlier on 6 June a section just for convoys had been set up at the Admiralty and it worked closely with the Intelligence Division and the Ministry of Shipping. Intelligence could quickly be relayed to convoy commodores by the wireless with which they were all now provided. Increasingly, the U-boats found the convoys more difficult to locate and attack and, as 1917 went on, the British introduced continual improvements and modifications in convoy efficiency. The introduction of airships, seaplanes and flying boats escorting convoys also proved a deterrent to the U-boats which were finding themselves short of targets. Associated factors were also important in counteracting the U-boats. Turnaround times to prevent congestion in Allied ports were shortened, for example, ships were concentrated on shorter routes and imports were restricted to concentrate on essential supplies. Over the summer of 1917, the British persisted with offensive tactics in conjunction with convoys. The results were paltry once again but they seemed reluctant to abandon them altogether. By the end of September, with the convoys reducing merchant losses, confidence began to grow and the Germans began to despair of breaking Britain through her commerce. In July and August only five vessels out of 800 convoyed had been lost. However, it should be noted that the number of ships lost overall was still higher than it had been before the introduction of unrestricted submarine warfare and, although there was reason for optimism, submarines would remain a threat until the end of the war.

Zeebrugge and Ostend

Discussions had long been held by the British to neutralise the ports of Zeebrugge and Ostend when they fell under German control and became the bases for their major force of submarines and for some light forces. In the summer of 1917, the War Committee decided that a major effort on land would be made in Flanders towards the ports and the navy was requested to mount a bombardment of them at the same time. Jellicoe was against the bombardment, believing that it could not be effective. In June and July, it was proposed that the Navy should land a division with tanks and artillery, although this was dependent upon Haig making sufficient advances on land. In the event, Haig was unable to break through on land and so the operation was cancelled in September. There was no real possibility of destroying the German U-boat flotillas and destroyers as they could easily hide in the maze of canals leading from Zeebrugge. In particular, Bruges, linked by canal to the port, was the perfect hiding place. Beatty, Bayly and Tyrwhitt had for some time had another idea to block Zeebrugge. The port was narrow and it was therefore feasible to block it and prevent the Germans from operating out of it. Roger Keyes had been keen on the idea since he became commander of the Dover Patrol and he submitted a proposal that was accepted at the end of February 1918.

Three obsolete cruisers were to be filled with cement and sunk at the main lock entrance to the mouth of the Zeebrugge-Bruges canal. At the same time another two blockships would be sunk at the entrance to Ostend harbour. To reach these targets the blockships had to get past a large stone mole that was connected to the shore with a viaduct forming the harbour, and then make their way to the canal entrance, a distance of over 3,000 metres.

The crew from the blockships would abandon ship once they were in place and would be picked up by a variety of small craft. There were batteries at the northern end of the mole that the raiding force would have to occupy while the operation took place in order to protect the blockships. The cruiser *Vindictive* would be adapted especially for the raid with machine guns, mortars, flame throwers and howitzers. Accompanying her would be two Mersey ferries that would carry long ladders in order to reach the mole. It was also planned that two obsolete submarines would be filled with explosives and blow themselves up under the viaduct so that it would be impossible for the Germans to reach the mole.

These were the central elements of the operation but it was also necessary to set up diversions. These were to be accomplished with the use of smokescreens, air attacks and bombardments of coastal batteries close to the ports by monitors. It was intended that the bombardments would start in the weeks prior to the main operation so that the Germans would be led to think of them as routine. The whole operation would require 165 vessels.

Keyes initially planned to go ahead in March but was forced to wait because there were insufficient chemicals to produce the smokescreen. His ships set sail on 11 April but were forced to turn back as initially there was almost no wind and then, when it did blow, it blew south so that the smokescreen would be ineffective and the ships exposed. Finally, they were able to go out on 23 April and, in view of the date, Keyes on the destroyer *Warwick* made the signal, 'St George for England', to which *Vindictive* replied, 'May we give the dragon's tail a damned good twist'.

The Germans had some warning of an impending attack, since plans had been discovered after the abortive attempt on 11 April, and they began to react shortly before *Vindictive* reached the mole. Much of the smokescreen was lost due to a change in wind direction and the destruction of some smoke floats by German guns. Gunfire rained down on the upper decks of *Vindictive* with a large number of casualties. In speeding up to try and avoid the guns, she also missed the intended landing point, with the result that the landing parties could not reach the battery, she could not cover them and she was exposed to batteries at the western part of the mole. Despite the difficulties, compounded by problems with anchoring, the landing parties got on to the mole although there was little that they could do. As the blockships entered the harbour, they re-embarked and, luckily, the *Vindictive* and the Mersey ferries escaped. One of the submarines made the viaduct, exploded and cut it off. The crew, although under heavy fire, escaped in a skiff. There was also some success with the blockships. Two of them made it to the canal entrance where they scuttled themselves as planned, although the third vessel sunk short of the entrance under German fire. The attempt on Ostend failed altogether because, once again, the smokescreen was rendered useless by the wind and, in addition, the Germans had deliberately moved the light buoy marking the harbour entrance so that the two blockships sank off target.

On 10 May, Keyes tried again to complete the plan at Ostend but one of the blockships had a problem with its boiler and, since she could only travel at 6 knots, had to fall back. The other made the harbour entrance but came under fire and grounded. The crew sunk her but in the wrong position. On the way back, *Warwick* was hit by a mine and was fortunate not to sink. She had to be towed back. Keyes intended to try again in June but this was cancelled when it seemed as if the Germans, in light of the bombardments, were no longer using Ostend. The apparent success at Zeebrugge did much for morale on the home front. Keyes was created a Knight Commander of the Bath and 11 VCs were awarded. How truly effective the blocking of Zeebrugge was is questionable. Ostend was not blocked and the canal from Bruges led there as well as Zeebrugge. Nevertheless, aerial photographs showed that German destroyers were holed up in Bruges and there were exposed submarines. Keyes now requested four aircraft squadrons to be placed under his command so that these could be attacked from the air. He received only a small proportion of what he had requested and consequently the air raids were not heavy enough or sustained for a long enough time to inflict real damage.

Overall, the Dover Patrol was successful in that after the raid there were no further attacks on the Dover barrage (a series of steel nets at varying heights anchored on the seabed to entrap submarines) and submarine traffic in the Dover Straits became negligible. German submarine losses began to rise due to successful convoys and counter measures and the east coast became increasingly dangerous for them. They were also under threat from the air and the potency of the Flanders flotillas was seriously undermined as 1918 proceeded. Almost continually throughout the war, the Dover Patrol had achieved its major objective of keeping the channels of communication with France open.

The Final Stages of War

In 1918, the High Seas Fleet would make one final sortie. Its target was the Scandinavian convoy which was protected by a detached battleship force. The British knew that the High Seas Fleet was still a threat and had anticipated possible attacks on the Dover barrage which did not materialise. However, Scheer imposed strict wireless silence on the plans for the convoy and, as a result, intelligence did not catch wind of the operation in advance. Hipper went out with the Second Scouting Group and the Second Flotilla on 23 April with backup from the High Seas Fleet. They were hampered by heavy fog at the Bight but they remained undetected and, on the morning of 24 April, they seemed to be well on course for a successful surprise attack. However, for all his meticulous planning, Scheer was let down by intelligence reports which had indicated the wrong sailing times for the convoy. There was no convoy for Scheer to intercept. He continued searching further north before turning back in the afternoon. Unfortunately for the Germans, the *Moltke* started to take on water after losing an inner screw and she was forced to break the radio silence before being taken under tow. Alerted, the Admiralty ordered Beatty to sea but there was no possibility of his ships being in time to intercept the High Seas Fleet. The Scandinavian convoy, however, had had a lucky escape.

As the war was coming to a close, aviation took on a more important role. Planes and flying boats had been increasingly used as part of submarine warfare and increasing numbers of vessels in the Grand Fleet were adapted with platforms for launching planes. At a conference in 1917, Beatty had made proposals to use Sopwith T.1 Cuckoo torpedo planes, along with flying boats, to attack the High Seas Fleet in port. However, there were simply not enough planes or carriers to mount the kind of operation that he envisaged and there was not yet the technical capacity for planes to carry an appropriate size of torpedo for the purpose. Beatty's grand plan was out of the question but there were smaller operations. In October 1918, for example, the newly commissioned *Argus*, a dedicated aircraft carrier, attacked the High Seas Fleet in Wilhelmshaven with the Sopwith T.1 Cuckoos. *Furious* was involved with air reconnaissance missions from the Bight which also destroyed a zeppelin shed at the base in Tondern. This was the first time that land planes had been flown off a carrier in a raid. It was the beginning of what would become an essential element of future naval warfare. Indeed, many of the lessons learnt would be invaluable during the Second World War. Those who had fought in the First World War would become the officers during the Second and, unlike their seniors in the earlier conflict, they would have experience of modern warfare and technology.

As the Allies were advancing into Belgium at the end of September, the German vessels evacuated the Flanders ports between 29 September and 3 October. Tyrwhitt had been on alert to intercept them leaving port but it seems that nobody expected them to leave so quickly and consequently the British were some hours behind the German fleet. Until the very end of the war, there was a possibility that the naval confrontation would end in a battle that would be the long-searched-for Trafalgar. It was not to be.

On 3 October, when Prince Max von Baden became German chancellor, he called for an armistice with President Wilson. The terms included a German withdrawal from enemy soil and a cessation of U-boat attacks on passenger vessels. Scheer was frustrated. While fighting was still going on, he was reluctant to put an end to the effectiveness of the submarine campaign. The Germans, now under immense pressure on the Western Front, were hoping for an all-out battle with the British Fleet and Scheer put together plans. British intelligence was aware of possible German moves to lure the Grand Fleet to the south. However, Scheer's plan, perceived as a suicidal mission, caused great unrest in an already demoralised German Fleet. On 29 October, when the German Fleet was ordered together at Schillig Roads, mutiny erupted.

When the armistice was signed on 11 November 1918, its naval terms stated that ten German dreadnoughts, six battle cruisers, eight light cruisers and fifty of the most modern destroyers were to be interned under care and maintenance parties at a designated Allied port. In addition, all submarines had to be surrendered, captured Russian warships had to be returned and the blockade would not be lifted until a peace treaty was signed. The Allied Naval Council agreed on Scapa Flow as the location for the interned German Fleet. In negotiations with Scheer's representative, Rear Admiral Meurer, it was decided that the submarines would surrender to Tyrwhitt at Harwich and the surface ships to Beatty in the Firth of Forth. They would then head for Scapa Flow and stay there until the peace treaty determined their ultimate fate.

On 20 November, the first submarines were escorted into port by Tyrwhitt who remained on action stations until they surrendered and ordered that there should be no cheering. Eventually 176 submarines were surrendered, including some that had been hiding in neutral ports. They would be shared out between the Allies. The German Fleet arrived in the Firth of Forth on 21 November, under the command of Rear Admiral von Reuter. Hipper was too heartbroken to take on the task. Beatty in the *Queen Elizabeth*, as well as around 370 ships representing other naval commands, met the German ships. The fleet was led through two columns of 13 British Squadrons by the light cruiser *Cardiff*. The columns then turned to escort them into port. Again the British remained on action stations in case the Germans attempted anything. At around 11am Beatty made the signal: 'The German flag will be hauled down at sunset today, Thursday, and will not be hoisted again without permission.' Famously Beatty told his fleet, 'I always told you they would have to come out.'

By June 1919, there was a still small German caretaker crew in Scapa Flow, as the fate of the vessels had still not been finalised for the peace treaty. On the morning of 21 June, when the British ships at Scapa went out on exercises, Reuter signalled his fleet to scuttle immediately. The British returned at full speed but virtually all the ships were destroyed; only the *Baden* and three cruisers were saved. It was an ignominious end for the fleet of which the Kaiser had been so proud. While the British appeared outraged there was probably also some relief in that it solved the problem of how the ships should be distributed amongst the Allies.

Although the war ended without a great victory in battle, it was nevertheless a great victory overall. It was the sustained blockade that gradually, but finally, forced the surrender of the Central Powers.

Profiles

Beatty, David, first Earl Beatty (1871–1936)

David Beatty was born in Cheshire on 17 January 1871, the son of Captain David Longfield Beatty of the 4th Hussars and his wife Katherine. A high-spirited boy, he joined the navy aged 13, entering the Royal Naval College, Dartmouth. He was appointed to the *Alexandra*, the flagship of the Mediterranean Fleet, rated midshipman in 1886 and was promoted to sub-lieutenant in 1890. In 1896–98, he served with distinction in the Sudan and in China during the Boxer Rebellion. In 1900, already marked out as a talented officer, he received one of four special promotions to captain, aged 29. The expected age for such a promotion was 42. He met his future wife, Ethel Field, while on leave in 1899 and they married in 1901 after she divorced her first husband. In June 1902, he took command of *Juno* with the Channel Fleet before being given command of the new cruiser *Suffolk* in the Mediterranean. Beatty became naval adviser to the Army council in 1906 and was involved in plans for transport of the BEF to France. Just before being promoted to Rear Admiral in 1910, Beatty served with the

Atlantic Fleet under Prince Louis of Battenberg. He turned down an appointment as second-in-command in the Atlantic, preferring the Home Fleet, which earned him some criticism, and unemployment until January 1912 when he was chosen by Churchill as naval secretary. In 1913, he was appointed Commander of the Grand Fleet's Battle Cruiser Squadron and that was the position he held at the outbreak of the War. He was involved in action at the Battles of Heligoland Bight, Dogger Bank and Jutland. In 1916, when Jellicoe was appointed First Sea Lord, Beatty took over as Commander-in-Chief of the Grand Fleet. He remained in this post until 1919, when he became First Sea Lord, the post he held until his retirement in 1927. He was also awarded an earldom and the Order of Merit in 1919. After retirement, he regularly spoke in the House of Lords, although he was not allied to any party. He died of heart failure in London on 12 March 1936.

Fisher, John Arbuthnot, first Baron Fisher (1841–1920)

John Fisher was the eldest child of Captain William Fisher of the 78th Highland Regiment and his wife Sophia and was born in Ceylon on 25 January 1841. His nomination to join the navy was from Admiral Sir William Parker, Nelson's last surviving captain. Fisher entered as a cadet on HMS *Calcutta*, sailing to the Baltic during the Crimean War, although, as the ship was powered solely by sail, he did not see action. After he was promoted to midshipman and joined *Highfligher* on the China Station, he first saw action at the Battle of Fatshan Creek and the capture of Canton in 1857. In 1861, he won the Beaufort Testimonial for his final examinations in navigation and was appointed to the gunnery school HMS *Excellent*. In 1863 he joined the first ironclad in the navy, HMS *Warrior*, as gunnery lieutenant. When he returned to *Excellent* in 1867, he developed his interest in torpedoes. Also during this period Fisher married Frances Broughton with whom he would have four children.

In 1869, he returned to the China Station as commander of the *Donegal*, before transferring to HMS *Ocean*. In 1872, back at *Excellent*, he was put in charge of torpedo instruction and promoted to captain in 1874. He was back at sea in 1876 in command of the *Pallas* in the Mediterranean Fleet and, in 1880, when the ship was paid off, he served as the president of a committee to revise the fleet's gunnery manual. April 1883 saw him back at *Excellent*, this time to command the gunnery school. In 1890, he gained promotion as rear admiral and took the position of admiral-superintendent of Portsmouth Dockyard. Fisher was made KCB in 1894, vice admiral in May 1896 and went back to sea as commander-in-chief in North America and the West Indies. By 1899, he had the premier command in the navy, commander-in-chief of the Mediterranean Fleet, becoming a full admiral in 1901 and Second Sea Lord in 1902. His long-held ambition was to be First Sea Lord which he achieved in 1904, presiding over the dreadnought building programme and naval reforms.

In 1905, he was promoted to admiral of the fleet and retired in 1910. Churchill recalled him in 1914 as First Sea Lord, as he had hoped, although both of them would lose their positions in 1915 over the disastrous Dardanelles and Gallipoli campaign. He then became chairman of the board of invention and research which was formed to engender scientific work for the navy. After the war, he worked on two volumes of his memoirs. He died of prostate cancer on 10 July 1920 in London.

Hipper, Franz von (1863–1932)

Franz von Hipper was born in Weilheim, Bavaria in 1863, and joined the German Imperial Navy in 1881 as cadet. He served on the frigates *Niobe* and *Leipzig* and commanded torpedo boats from 1888 to 1903. In 1912 and 1913, he led the High Seas Fleet Scouting Forces and, on the outbreak of war, he led his battle cruisers on several raids on British coastal towns. He played major roles in the Battle of Dogger Bank and, more particularly, in the Battle of Jutland. He was knighted by King Ludwig III of Bavaria after Jutland. In 1918, he was promoted to Admiral and took over from Scheer as commander-in-chief of the High Seas Fleet. He had the unenviable task of organising the surrender of the High Seas Fleet to the British at the end of the war and retired from service in November 1918. He lived out the rest of his life in Othmarschen near Hamburg and died in 1932.

Jellicoe, John Rushworth, first Earl Jellicoe (1859–1935)

Jellicoe was the second son of John Henry Jellicoe, a captain in the Royal Mail Steam Packet Company, and his wife Lucy Henrietta. He was born on 5 December 1859 in Southampton. In 1872, he joined the Navy as a cadet on the training ship HMS *Britannia*, passing out top of his term in 1874. His first appointment as midshipman was with the flying squadron on the frigate *Newcastle*. In 1877, he was appointed to the *Agincourt*, initially based with the Channel Fleet and then the Mediterranean Fleet. In 1880, he was promoted and came home to specialise in gunnery and the following year he spent another spell on *Agincourt* before attending the Royal Naval College, Greenwich. In 1884, he qualified as a gunnery lieutenant and was appointed to the staff of the gunnery school *Excellent*, under John Fisher who would have a major influence on his career. He was Fisher's personal staff officer when Fisher was flag captain to Admiral Hornby in the Baltic Fleet in 1885 and, in 1889, when Fisher was director of naval ordnance, Jellicoe became his assistant. In 1891, he was promoted to commander and became the executive officer of the *Pareil* in the Mediterranean Fleet, later moving to the flagship *Victoria*. When he returned to England in 1896, he was promoted to captain and was appointed to the ordnance committee. He went back to sea in 1897 to the China Station in *Centurion*, returning to the Admiralty in 1902 as assistant to the Third Sea Lord, Admiral William May. The same year he married Florence Gwendoline Cayzer. He commanded the cruiser *Drake* before becoming director of naval ordnance in 1904. He was made a CVO in this period for his work on the development of HMS *Dreadnought* and, in 1907, became a rear admiral and was appointed second-in-command of the Atlantic Fleet. It was just a year before he was back at the Admiralty as controller by which time he had been knighted and created a KCVO. He was given command of the Atlantic Fleet in 1910, as acting vice admiral, and the following year he was second-in-command of the Home Fleet, before becoming Second Sea Lord in 1912. When war broke out in 1914, he was appointed commander-in-chief of the Grand Fleet, which he reluctantly left in 1916 to become First Sea Lord. After the war, he received many decorations at home and abroad, including being made Viscount Jellicoe of Scapa and the GVCO. He also wrote his memoirs of the war and was sent to the dominions as an advisor for their navies. He was replaced by Beatty as First Sea Lord in 1919, when there was controversy over the conduct of Jutland. Between 1920 and 1924 he was governor-general of New Zealand and was made an earl on his return. Back in Britain, he remained active, working for the London County Council, the Boy Scouts, the Empire Service League, the National Rifle Association and as president of the British Legion until his death from pneumonia on 19 November 1935.

Keyes, Roger John Brownlow, first Baron Keyes
(1872–1945)

Roger Keyes was the second son of Brigadier Sir Charles Patton Keyes and Katherine Jessie. He was born on 4 October 1872 at Tundiani Fort in India where his father was commander of the Punjab frontier force. He joined the navy as a cadet at the Royal Naval College, Dartmouth in 1885. In 1887, he joined HMS *Raleigh* on the Africa station. He was made sub-lieutenant in 1892, serving with the Channel Fleet on the armoured cruiser *Immortalitie*, and then on the royal yacht *Victoria and Albert*. He was promoted to lieutenant on the sloop *Beagle*, serving in South America between 1893 and 1896 before returning to England. He gained his first command in 1897, on the destroyer *Opossum* in the Devenport Instructional Flotilla, followed in 1898 with command of the *Hart* on the China station. He was involved in resisting Chinese forces on the Kowloon peninsula, a cutting-out expedition on the Beihe River and campaigns in Beijing. He was promoted to the rank of commander in November 1900, having already proved himself willing to take on responsibility and gained reputation for using his initiative. From 1901–1903, he was second-in-command of the Devenport Destroyer Flotilla before serving in naval intelligence and becoming the naval attaché to Italy and Austria-Hungary between 1905 and 1908. He was promoted to captain in 1905. In 1906, he married Eva Mary Salvin with whom he would have two sons and three daughters. In 1908–10, he commanded *Venus* with the Atlantic Fleet before being appointed inspecting captain of submarines, and then commodore in charge of the Submarine Service in 1912. He was still in this command at the outbreak of the First World War and took to sea as often as possible. Together with Reginald Tyrwhitt, he was instrumental in the planning for the Battle of Heligoland Bight. He then became chief of staff firstly to Vice Admiral Carden, who was in command of the naval forces off the Dardanelles, and then to De Robeck when he replaced Carden. He followed De Robeck to Salonika when a new front was opened in an effort to save Serbia. In June 1916, he was given command of the battleship *Centurion* in the 2nd battle squadron of the Grand Fleet and promoted to rear admiral in 1917. He then became second-in-command in the 4th battle squadron on *Colossus*. He was appointed director of plans at the Admiralty in September 1917. He was created a KCB for his part in the plans for the raid on Zeebrugge and Ostend. At the end of the war he was created a KCVO and made a baronet in 1919. Keyes took command of the battle cruiser squadron between 1919 and 1921 before becoming the deputy chief of naval staff and, in 1925, commander-in-chief of the Mediterranean station. His last appointment came in 1929 as commander-in-chief, Portsmouth, during which period, in 1930, he was made admiral of the fleet. He was, however, disappointed not to be appointed as First Sea Lord. In retirement, he became a Conservative MP from 1934 until 1943 when he was made a peer. He also wrote accessible accounts of his action in the First World

War. During the Second World War, Churchill appointed Keyes as director of combined operations in 1940. It was a difficult time for him with many of his plans rejected and deteriorating relationships with chiefs of staff and, in 1941, he was replaced. Nevertheless, he was made a baron in 1943 and took diplomatic missions to the USA, Australia and New Zealand. He died at home in Buckinghamshire on 26 December 1945 and was remembered as a man of action and spirit.

Scheer, Admiral Reinhardt (1863–1928)

Scheer was born in Obernkirchen, Hanover in 1863 and entered the German navy in 1879. In the 1890s, he gained a reputation as a torpedo specialist and he was promoted to the rank of captain in 1907. He married Emilie Mohr in 1899, who was murdered during an attempted robbery of their home in 1920. In 1910, he was appointed chief of staff to the High Seas Fleet, becoming commander of the Second Battle Squadron in 1913. He was a strategist in the use of submarine warfare and planned many of the submarine raids on the English coastline during World War One. He was made commander of the High Seas Fleet in 1916 and played a prominent part in the Battle of Jutland. In August 1918, Scheer became head of the Naval Supreme Command and planned a last ditch attempt on the Grand Fleet but the navy saw this as suicidal and it prompted mutiny. The plan came to nothing. The Kaiser removed him from office in November 1918 and he retired a month later. After the war he published his memoirs of the High Seas Fleet. He died in Marktredwitz on 26 November 1928.

Spee, Admiral Maximilian von (1861–1914)

Maximilian von Spee was born in Copenhagen and joined the Imperial German Navy in 1878. In 1887 he was appointed in command of the ports in the German colony of Cameroon and served there until 1888 before working in weapons development. In 1908, he became chief of staff for the North Sea and was promoted to rear admiral in 1910. In 1912, Spee became commander of the East Asian Squadron and, from the moment war broke out, terrorized British merchant vessels in the area. He also played a prominent role in the Battle of Coronel and the Battle of the Falkland Islands. At the Battle of the Falklands Spee's flagship *Scharnhorst* was sunk and he was killed.

Tirpitz, Admiral Alfred von (1849–1930)

Tirpitz was the son of a civil servant and joined the Prussian Navy in 1865, receiving his first commission in 1869. He became interested in the potential of the submarine in warfare when he served as the commander of a torpedo flotilla and he subsequently became inspector general of the torpedo fleet. In 1895, he was promoted to Rear Admiral and served firstly in East Asia with a cruiser squadron from 1896, before becoming Secretary of State of the Imperial Navy Department the following year. Tirpitz shared the Kaiser's vision for a much larger German fleet and they worked closely together. Tirpitz was largely responsible for the First Fleet Act in 1898 which legislated for the reorganisation and considerable expansion of the navy. It was followed, in 1900, by another act that was much more ambitious, giving the scope to build a fleet that would be a match for the Royal Navy. In 1911, he was made Grand Admiral and became Commander of the German Navy when war broke out in 1914. He was very much in favour of unrestricted submarine warfare which strained diplomatic relations with Germany. When this led to limited submarine warfare, Tirpitz resigned in 1916, although he was surprised that the Kaiser accepted his resignation. After the war, he became leader of the right-wing Fatherland Party and was a Deputy in the Reichstag from 1924 to 1928. He died in Ebenhausen near Munich in 1930.

Tyrwhitt, Sir Reginald Yorke (1870–1951)

Tyrwhitt was born on 10 May 1870, the fifth son of Reverend Richard St John Tyrwhitt and the fourth with his second wife Caroline. He started as a naval cadet, joining *Britannia* in Dartmouth in 1883. He subsequently served on the *Australia* and *Ajax,* gaining promotion to lieutenant in 1892, when he was appointed to the light cruiser *Cleopatra* stationed in North America. In 1896, he was given command of the *Hart*, an early destroyer and, at the end of that year, he became 1st lieutenant on the commander-in-chief's yacht on the Mediterranean before taking up a similar position in North America. In 1903, he married Sarah Corbally with whom he would have one son and two daughters. Also in 1903 he gained promotion to commander and was commissioned to *Aurora*, a tender boat to the *Britannia*. He went on to command the destroyer *Waveney* in 1904–5, and two scout vessels *Attentive* and *Skirmisher* in 1906 and 1907 respectively. He was made captain in 1908 and took command of the destroyer *Topaze* for two years before being made flag captain under Sir Douglas Gamble on the Mediterranean station, first on the *Bacchante* and then on *Good Hope*. In 1912, he returned to Britain to captain the second destroyer flotilla of the Home Fleet and was promoted to commodore in 1914, in charge of all destroyer squadrons. For the duration of the First World War, Tyrwhitt was based with the Harwich Force and was made rear-admiral in 1918. He was a highly effective war leader and jointly planned the action at Heligoland Bight with Roger Keyes. After the action, he was created CB and later, in 1917, KCB. In 1916, he was also awarded a DSO. As well as being a specialist with destroyers, he was also keen on the use of aircraft within the navy and provided the cover for the seaplane raid on zeppelin sheds at the end of 1914. He was involved with the action at Dogger Bank and many other smaller scale operations with the Harwich force and the Dover patrol. When the war ended, it was Tyrwhitt who accepted the surrender of the German submarines. After the war he was made a baronet, received many foreign decorations and an honorary degree from Oxford. He was appointed as the senior officer in Gibraltar and, in 1921, took command of the Third Light Cruiser Squadron in the Mediterranean. Between 1923 and 1929 he held various appointments as commanding officer of the coast of Scotland, admiral superintendent of the Rosyth Dockyard, and commander-in-chief of the China Station. After service in China he was promoted to both admiral and GCB. In 1930–33, he was commander-in-chief at the Nore and the principle aide-de-camp to the King in 1932. In 1934, he became admiral of the fleet. He was 70 at the outbreak of the Second World War and served in the Home Guard. He died on 30 May 1951 at Ellenden, Sandhurst, Kent.

Chronology

1914

4 August
Britain declares war on Germany.
Goeben and *Breslau* bombard the French Algerian ports of
Bone and Philippeville.
Admiral Jellicoe takes over as Commander-in-Chief of the
Grand Fleet.
28 August
The Battle of Heligoland Bight.
30 October
Fisher returns as First Sea Lord.
1 November
The Battle of Coronel.
3 November
British and French bombard the Dardanelles.
Germans bombard Great Yarmouth and Gorleston.
8 December
The Battle of the Falklands.

1915

24 January

The Battle of Dogger Bank.

18 February

British waters declared as an unrestricted war zone by Germany.

19 February

British and French begin bombardment of Dardanelles forts.

18 March

British and French enter the Dardanelles.

7 May

Lusitania sunk by a U-boat.

17 May

Fisher resigns as First Sea Lord.

28 May

Admiral Sir Henry Jackson becomes First Sea Lord.

19 December

Evacuation from Gallipoli begins, ending on 9 January 1916.

1916

23 February

German submarine campaign resumed in British waters.

1 May

Submarine campaign extended to the western Atlantic.

31 May
The Battle of Jutland.
26 October
Raid on the Dover barrage.

1917

11 March
British forces take Baghdad.
4 May
First American naval vessels arrive at Queenstown to assist convoys.
26 November
Official formation of the WRNS.

1918

1 April
Founding of the RAF.
12 April
Grand Fleet moves base to Rosyth.
23 April
British attack Zeebrugge and Ostend.
19 July
Air attack on Tondern.
21 October
Submarine campaign on commerce stops.
11 November
Armistice.

1919

21 June
German fleet scuttles itself at Scapa Flow.

Selected Bibliography

Gordon, Andrew, *The Rules of the Game: Jutland and British Naval Command*, London: John Murray, 1996.

Readable, detailed account of Jutland.

Halpern, Paul, *A Naval History of World War I,* London: UCL Press, 1994.

Probably the most comprehensive account, very detailed and aimed at the academic reader.

Hough, Richard, *The Great War at Sea 1914–1918,* Oxford: OUP, 1983.

Densely written but readable account.

Howard, Michael, *The First World War,* Oxford, OUP, 2002.

Excellent short overview of the War for the beginner, although scant coverage of naval aspects.

Osborne, Eric. W, *The Battle of Heligoland Bight,* Bloomington: Indiana University Press, 2006.

Analysis of the Battle of Heligoland Bight aimed at the academic reader.

Preston, Diana, *Wilful Murder: The Sinking of the Lusitania*, London: Black Swan, 2003.

Fascinating and compelling account of the sinking of the *Lusitania* and the events around it.

Thompson, Julian, *The Imperial War Museum Book of the War at Sea 1914–1918,* London: Pan, 2006.
Compelling account of the war at sea, illustrated with first hand testimonies.
Wragg, David, *Royal Navy Handbook 1914–1918,* Stroud: Sutton Publishing, 2006.
A good general overview of the world at sea, particularly good for appendices of warships and medals.

Index

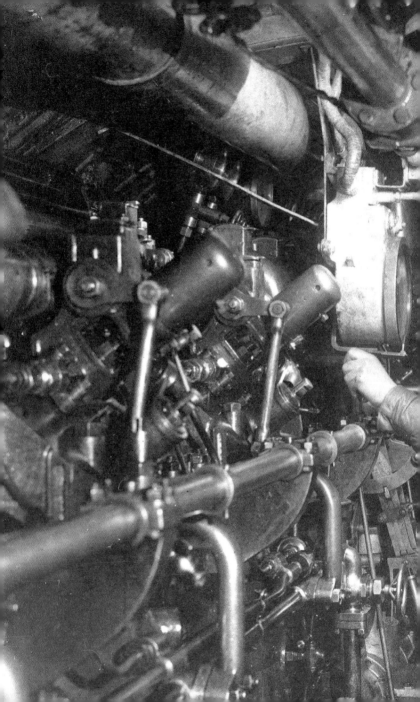